Creature Comforts

Creature Comforts

SYLVIA FENTON

Illustrated by David Astin

London
GEORGE ALLEN & UNWIN
Boston   Sydney

George Allen & Unwin (Publishers) Ltd,
40 Museum Street, London WC1A 1LU, UK

George Allen & Unwin (Publishers) Ltd,
Park Lane, Hemel Hempstead, Herts HP2 4TE, UK

Allen & Unwin Inc.,
Fifty Cross Street, Winchester, Mass 01890, USA

George Allen & Unwin Australia Pty Ltd,
8 Napier Street, North Sydney, NSW 2060, Australia

First published in 1985

British Library Cataloguing in Publication Data

Fenton, Sylvia
    Creature comforts.
1. Animal culture
I. Title
636.08'3   SF61
ISBN 0–04–925033–7

Set in 11 on 13 point Plantin by
Nene Phototypesetters Ltd, Northampton
and printed in Great Britain
Anchor Brendon Limited, Tiptree, Essex

CHAPTER 1

From his perch by the window Wol watches with saucer-wide eyes as I clear the clutter from the table and get out typewriter and paper. His fat little body quivering with curiosity, he scuttles from one end of the perch to the other and back again, frantically trying to find the best vantage point. Craning his head at an angle of about 270 degrees, he hangs upside-down in an effort to get a better view. His greatest fear is that he might miss something. When I sit down at the table it is too much for him; he is not used to my sitting down during the day and his worst suspicions are confirmed – something's up! Deciding that this calls for closer investigation, he swoops down from his perch, landing accurately – and painfully – on my head. He follows every move closely. Cover off typewriter, nod, nod. Put paper in typewriter, nod, nod. Strike key – good gracious, what was that? He hops onto the roller and inspects what I have written – half a word, so far – decides that he doesn't like it and methodically shreds the paper to ribbons. I control my immediate impulse, which is to strangle him, and count to ten. A bad strategy, as it turns out, as this gives him ample time to reduce the typewriter ribbon to spaghetti.

I decide the time has come for a showdown and, lifting him onto my lap, look him straight in the eye. Intrigued by this turn of events and wondering what on earth is coming next, he looks straight back. Having captured his attention I explain the economic facts of life to him: that liver and beef and mealworms and such-like Wol-relishing goodies do not grow on trees; they have to be bought. With money. Money also does not grow on trees; it has to be earned. Which I am trying to do by writing his story. So it would be much appreciated if he would kindly direct his attentions elsewhere and let me get on with it. He listens enthralled to all this, punctuating every other word with enthusiastic head-nodding, and I am much encouraged. I change the ribbon and put another sheet of paper in the typewriter, watched intently by a subdued and penitent Wol. I strike a key. He hops onto the roller and without even bothering to read what I have written this time, repeats his shredding act. A stifled scream escapes me. Wol, concerned, hops onto my shoulder and sticks his woolly little head into my mouth – Did you make that funny noise? 'All right,' I say to him, 'you are apparently not motivated by material rewards, but what about fame? If I write your story you will be famous. Everyone will know what an enchanting, intelligent, charismatic little owl you are. How does that grab you?' Clearly, it doesn't. He hops back onto the typewriter and expresses his opinion, very graphically and exceedingly messily, all over the keyboard. I know when I'm beaten; I put him back on his perch, clean up the typewriter and put it away. Wol's story, and the story of all the other waifs who have taken up residence since I moved into the cottage, will have to wait until Wol is in bed.

The still, small voice of conscience nags me: 'There

2

are other rooms in the cottage. You don't have to work under Wol's beady eye.' True enough. Perhaps I am using Wol as an excuse not to work. I consider the various alternatives. The sitting room is definitely out; I'm pretty sure that the convalescent buzzard recuperating in there would agree with me that the room ain't big enough for the both of us. The cloakroom is too small, and in any case the only place to sit, the loo seat, already has a sitting tenant – a squirrel with a broken leg. Upstairs then – the bedroom? No fear – not with three baby kestrels on the windowsill who are conditioned to open their mouths and squawk for food every time I hove into view. I couldn't see them letting me waste my time working when I could be more usefully occupied shoving disgusting bits of shredded beef garnished with chopped feathers down their ever-open gullets. The bathroom? You must be joking. The noise level from the pair of loud-mouthed ducklings in there is only marginally below that of a pneumatic drill. And in any case I don't think I could bear to watch what they're doing to my lovely shiny new bath.

That just leaves the study. Ah, my lovely study. When the designer and I were drawing up the plans for the cottage conversion we very nearly came to blows over the study. 'You can't be serious,' he gasped. 'If you have a study that means you'll only have one bedroom!' 'So?' I replied. 'I'm only one person. I only need one bedroom.' 'But what if anyone wants to stay?' he pleaded. 'There'll be nowhere to put them.' 'Yes, I know,' I said, 'isn't it lovely?' I'd had my fill of fair-weather friends when I was living in the caravan. Right through the winter, when I could have done with a hand shovelling snow and hauling bales of hay up on a sledge there was nary a peep out of them. Came the first day of spring and suddenly I was the most popular

3

person around. Hordes of pasty-faced townies, some of whom I scarcely knew, came swarming up the path twittering on about how terribly worried they'd been about me during this dreadful winter, couldn't wait another minute to reassure themselves that I was all right. How very heart-warming, I thought, as I bustled around whipping up an ad-hoc meal out of a superannuated lump of cheese, two senile tomatoes and whatever I could purloin in the way of eggs from my miserly hens, and tripping over their elegantly nyloned legs every time I turned round. 'Oh, sweetie, you shouldn't have bothered for us,' they chirruped when I served up my pathetic odds-and-sods omelette. 'We ate on the way here' – then set to with gusto demolishing the lot. Occasionally one, more discerning than the rest, would murmur sympathetically, 'You look harassed, my love, it's all too much for you, this pioneer, back-to-the-roots lark. We did warn you, didn't we?

When eventually they left it was with much commiseration 'at leaving you alone. Never mind, when you're in the cottage we'll be able to stay longer.' Like hell you will, I thought. So the designer's pleas for a second bedroom cut very little ice with me – it was going to be a study or nothing. Not that it made a scrap of difference, as it turned out. I'd hardly been in the cottage five minutes before visitors started turning up, unheralded and uninvited, at the crack of dawn – 'Might as well make a day of it.' – getting under my feet and keeping me from doing the several thousand things I had to do. As day turned into night and they made no attempt to go I started dropping oblique hints about time getting on, got to get up early in the morning, heavy day tomorrow, which were completely ignored. So were more direct ones such as 'I don't know about you, but I'm ready for bed' and 'You've got a long drive ahead of you, shouldn't you be making a move?' Finally I played my ace in the hole: 'I'd love you to stay the night but I haven't got a spare room.' 'Oh, don't worry about us, poppet' they carolled, 'We'll doss down on the floor.'

Grouchily lugging blankets and pillows downstairs, rearranging furniture to make room for these layabouts and surveying the living room, which was fast taking on the appearance of a gipsy encampment, it occurred to me that I had been a bit too clever for my own good. It would have been a darn sight easier to have shoved them all into a spare room and shut the door on them. Bidding them a solicitous good-night I made my way upstairs, appalled at my own hypocrisy; I knew there was no way they could have a good night, not once the feline gang-of-five discovered their presence. Banned from the upstairs rooms, the cats were suffering a deep sense of deprivation. To find sundry warm human bodies lying around on their patch would be tantamount to stumbling across the keys of heaven so far as they were concerned.

I couldn't believe the scene that confronted me when, somewhat mellowed after a good night's sleep, I came downstairs the next morning The room looked as though it had been hit by a hurricane. Half-naked contorted bodies sprawled in abandon all over the floor and pillows and blankets were scattered thither and yon. Randomly distributed over the recumbent bodies were five deliriously happy cats, blissfully purring their heads off as they kneaded their hosts' midriffs with needle-sharp claws. Clearly there had been a confrontation during the night between dossers and cats. I know who my money was on! 'Morning all,' I trilled brightly. 'Sleep well?' A jaundiced eye opened and a faltering hand reached out for a pillow to throw. I beat a hasty retreat.

OK, I told myself, so you've been hoist by your own petard. Perhaps a spare bedroom wouldn't have been such a bad idea. But I loved my study. Every day I went in there, shut the door and just stood admiring it. The super leather-topped desk, the executive-type swivel chair, the impressive cupboards and bookshelves, all courtesy of local auctions. I went over to the window and gloried in the view – the sweep of the field down into the valley, donkeys grazing in the paddock, cats playing silly fools in the garden, ducks, geese and hens going industriously about their business. It was all so beautiful – and it was all mine! It was a wonderful room for meditation, but as a workroom it was a dead loss. Time that should have been spent working was frittered away gazing through the window at the goings-on

outside and wishing I was there. All the action was downstairs, and here was I, isolated and cut off from it all. It wasn't fair! Some people can only work in a peaceful atmosphere, but I'm not one of them. Give me a cluttered room full of cats and other itinerants, with the radio or television going and a minor crisis cropping up ever half hour or so and just watch me go. Unfortunately, I didn't discover this until too late, when the study was a fait accompli. I was in real trouble now – I couldn't work in the study because it was too quiet, and I couldn't work anywhere else because I was too guilt-ridden about the study going to waste. As it turned out, the problem resolved itself. A steady stream of orphaned and injured creatures started arriving and in no time at all I found myself running out of places to put them. So, with an enormous sense of relief tinged with just the merest touch of martyrdom, I turned the study into a casualty ward.

In summer the turnover of furred and feathered foundlings is fairly brisk so space, or rather the lack of it, isn't much of a problem, particularly as the convalescents can be housed outside when the weather is fine. But winter is an absolute nightmare because, even when they are well again, the birds can't be released until the weather turns warmer. So there were times, particularly during the first winter in the cottage when I wasn't yet properly organised, when every room was filled to overflowing and I seriously (well, semi-seriously) considered handing the place over to the birds and beasts and moving back into the caravan. This would have suited the cats very well indeed. After almost two years in the caravan they were nicely settled in and saw no reason why they should be expected to disrupt their life-style simply because I had taken it into my head to move all of fifteen yards away into a place

7

smelling disagreeably of paint, turpentine and new-
ness. They made it quite clear that so far as they were
concerned, I could please myself but speaking personally they had absolutely no intention of coming with
me. 'It's customary to wait until you're asked,' I
informed them, playing it cool. I wasn't worried
because, as food-provider, I knew I held the trump
card. 'Come supper time they'll soon change their
minds,' I told myself. But they didn't. After half an
hour I went outside and called them. 'Food, puddies.
Come and get it.' Five woebegone furry faces appeared
at the carvan window. I rattled the food dishes; they
looked interested but didn't budge. 'OK, play it your
way,' I said, and went back into the cottage confident
that they'd soon follow.

By midnight I had resigned myself to the fact that,
unbelievably, their principles were apparently stronger
than their appetites. The urge to go over to the caravan
and plead with them to come back with me was
overwhelming, but I resisted it. I too have my pride!
But when breakfast time came and went and still no
sign of them I thought, 'To hell with pride!' and went
across to the caravan, threw open the door and said, 'All
right, enough of this nonsense. Are you coming back
with me or not?' They regarded me with mournful eyes
and mewed piteously, 'Come back with you? In our
condition? We haven't got the strength to get down off
the bed, let alone walk anywhere.' So that's the way it
is, I thought. I expected a touch of the martyrs from
Rufus, the senior cat – he's got it down to a fine art, but
I was a bit surprised to see the rest of them trying it on.
Well, it won't wash, I decided. I left them to it and went
back to the cottage. But I couldn't settle to anything –
apart from anything else, I missed them. After living
cheek by paw with five cats for so long I felt dreadfully

8

isolated rattling around in the comparative vastness of the cottage on my own.

By the supper time I could stand it no longer. I made up a tray and took it across to the caravan. They watched impassively as I set their dishes down on the floor but made no attempt to get stuck in. Not even Pudding, who can best be described as an appetite on legs. They turned tragedy-laden eyes on me: 'It's too late now, we're too weak even to eat'. 'Well, it's there if you want it,' I told them. 'Try to force yourselves.' Closing the door behind me I crept round to the side window and peered through; five cats, miraculously recovered, were ranged around the dishes, slurping back their food with complete abandon.

And so the pattern was set. Three times a day I trudged across to the caravan with their tray, bitterly regretting my weakness. Now I'd never get them to come and live in the cottage. I had visions of myself in ten, twenty years time, old and wizened, back bent as I hobbled over to the caravan clutching a tray in twisted, arthritic fingers. 'By that time I'll probably qualify for meals on wheels myself,' I thought sourly. Sitting by the fire in my comfortable living room on the third day I found I couldn't rid my mind of the picture of five shivering cats, abandoned and unloved, sinking into a decline in a cold dark caravan. I went into the barn and started up the generator so that they'd have light, then dug out the paraffin heater that I'd abandoned so joyously only days before and took it over to the caravan. The cats watched smugly as I set it down and lit it: 'We knew you'd see sense sooner or later. Isn't it better here?' I looked around the room that had been my home for the past twenty months. It had a comfortable familiarity about it, a lived-in look that the cottage hadn't yet acquired. For a moment or two I was tempted, 'just for ten minutes or so,' to keep the cats company. Suddenly the sheer lunacy of the situation struck me. Really, I was no better than the cats, clinging to the old and familiar just because it *was* familiar. I hotfooted it back to the cottage.

After about a week of keeping two homes going I had just about given up all hope of ever persuading the cats to join me when the breakthrough came. There was a rattle of the cat-flap and a little pink snout peered through. After a quick recce of the kitchen the rest of Charlie followed. 'Hallo Charlie', I said, not wanting to make too big a deal of it, 'just in time for supper,' and I opened the fridge. Dead on cue Pudding squeezed through the flap, followed in short order by Flossie and Min. I shovelled out their food and, while they were tucking in, went in search of Rufus. He was sitting bolt upright in the middle of the caravan, mewing querulously. He was old and fragile and everybody had abandoned him. He would die alone, unloved and unmourned. I knew it was no use trying to coax him, he was enjoying his martyrdom too much to relinquish it voluntarily, so I picked him up and carried him back to the cottage. And at long last I could shut the door of the caravan for good.

My own move into the cottage had not been without incident. All the structural work had been done and all that remained was the painting, so it looked as though I'd be able to move in within a couple of weeks. And then, on the day he was due to start, the painter came  down with flu. I responded in the only possible way in the circumstances – I had hysterics. The builder was most put out at this uncharacteristic behaviour; having taken all the previous crises in my stride, he considered it most unreasonable of me to throw a fit over what was, after all, no more than a hiccup. 'It might be a hiccup to you,' I screamed, 'To me, it's the last straw.' He explained that everything was under control, he had arranged to borrow a painter from another building firm. This struck me as most odd – a builder loaning one of his men to a competitor. Such altruism! Altruism? More like sabotage, as it turned out. I could just picture the scene in the rival builder's office:

Gaffer: Just had Bert Willen on the blower. Wants to borrow a painter. Who we got?

Foreman: Well, there's Arthur. He'll be finished that pub job by tomorrow.

Gaffer: You gone barmy or something? I don't want Michaelengo, I just want someone who can slap on a coat or two.

Foreman: What about young Billy . . . ?

Gaffer: Nah, he's started cleaning his brushes between colours, that makes him a craftsman.

Foreman: Well, that only leaves Harry. He's got nothing on since that old bag in the bungalow slung him out for painting her carpets and mixing his paint in her teapot.

Gaffer: Harry – yeah, he'll do fine.

So I got Harry, and the worst paint job on record. He was a one-brush man; one brush for the undercoat, the top coat, gloss paint, emulsion, walls and windows, inside and out. As he never cleaned his brush between operations ('I like a nice weathered brush') I finished up with some extremely unorthodox colour and texture combinations. He was also a firm believer in 'leaving things like nature intended', so none of the new wood was prepared before painting. As a result resin oozed

11

out of the untreated knotholes and bled through the paint. When I asked him why he hadn't treated the knot holes he replied, 'Well, if they're not holes I can't see much point in treating them.' As somebody once said, there's no answer to that. But the really final straw came when I investigated three odd-looking bumps on the kitchen windowsill and discovered that he'd painted over two moths and a ladybird. 'I didn't have the heart to disturb them,' he informed me virtuously when I taxed him with it. I slung him out and finished the painting myself.

Living in the caravan hadn't been exactly a barrel of laughs; each day had brought its quota of problems but those I couldn't solve I learned to live with. After all, it was only a temporary measure – once I was in the cottage all these problems would disappear. Which they did, only to be replaced by a whole lot of new, cottage-related ones. When I first told my London friends that I was planning to live in the country they did everything possible to discourage me. They catalogued all the negative aspects of country living – the mud, the isolation, the bitterly cold winters, the lack of facilities, the bugs. None of these things put me off. But if they had said 'septic tanks' I might well have thought again. Living in town the question of what is euphemistically referred to as 'waste disposal' hadn't exercised my thoughts all that much – you just pulled the handle and that was the end of it. Now, for the first time, I was brought face to face with the nitty-gritty of the whole business and I didn't much like it. Not to put too fine a point on it, I found that when I pulled the handle not a lot happened. With some problems a 'take no notice and it will go away' philosophy sometimes works, but this definitely wasn't one of them. I rang the local council and told them I was having trouble with my septic tank; 'We'll send someone along to look into it,' they promised, which struck me as not the most fortunate choice of words in the circumstances. An official duly arrived and poured some purple dye into the tank. After flushing the loo we both stood entranced, watching as a purple stain appeared on the ground and rapidly spread down the bank into the next field where it lay in a limpid, highly coloured pool. 'You're quite right,' said the effluent disposal expert with great perspicacity, 'It is oozing out.' He diagnosed a build-up of sludge over the years and said arrangements would be made for someone to come and empty the tank.

Two days later an enormous tanker rattled up the path and out climbed Mr Sludge. Everything about him was sludge coloured – his hair, his clothes, even his face. The only discordant note was his hands; they were encased in a pair of shocking-pink rubber gloves, giving an air of vulgar refinement to the overall picture. Mr Sludge himself was an absolute joy – a man in love with life, with himself and, especially, with his work. Sewage was in his blood and he related to it on a personal level, always referring to it as 'she' which, if I were more of a feminist, I might have taken exception to. But his joy and delight in his work were so contagious that I took it as a compliment to my sex! I left him joyfully wallowing and went inside to put the kettle on. 'Come in when you're ready for your tea,' I told him. After half an hour I went to look for him; he was standing entranced, watching the last dregs of sludge slurping away. 'Tea's ready,' I said. He turned an enraptured face to me. 'There she goes,' he breathed reverently. 'That be the last of her.' And with a sigh of deep content he started packing away his equipment.

As we went into the cottage I pointed the way to the

cloakroom so that he could wash his hands. 'Oh, no need for that, old dear! That's why I wear the gloves, see, to keep my hands clean.' And, unbelievably, he started tucking into tea and cakes with his gloves still on. Try as I might, I couldn't take my eyes off those bright pink sausages on the ends of his arms. Like the mother in the story who, having warned her small child not to mention the vicar's outsize nose when he came to tea, found herself asking her guest 'Do you take milk and sugar in your nose?' I heard myself, to my horror saying, 'Try one of these pink gloves, I made them myself.' Conversation was difficult enough as it was; every comment I made was greeted with a knowing wink, a finger laid against the nose and a rustic rhyme. 'Wonder if it'll stay dry,' I said idly. 'When the moon is on the wane/Chances are we'll get some rain.' he responded. 'Blowing up a bit,' I offered hopefully. 'The wicked east wind blows and blows/Giving you a runny nose,' Then, to make sure he'd covered all the options, 'When the wind is in the west/Maids and youths should wear a vest.' Vests? Runny noses? Was this the language of our yeoman forebears? My suspicions that he was a bit of a phoney were strengthened by his solemn assurance that 'If the cuckoo calls at night/ Weather next day will be bright.' 'I've never heard a cuckoo call at night!' I protested. 'No more have I, my duck' said he 'but it's the only thing that rhymes.' 'You old fraud,' I cried, 'You're making them up!' 'Well, of course I am' he replied. 'I'm a poet.' He finished his tea and after fastidiously wiping his pink-gloved fingers on a scrap of dun-coloured rag, made for the door. 'See you in about six months' time, I called after him. 'Don't leave it no longer,' he warned, 'If cess pools aren't emptied of'en/Fumes arise and start you coughin'. Beat that for an exit line, I thought.

14

CHAPTER 2

Not long after I moved into the cottage the first casualty arrived. Alec, from the farm across the field, turned up on the doorstep covered in blood and at first I thought he was the patient until I saw the bundle of gory feathers in his hand. Alec laid the bird on the kitchen table and after cleaning off as much of the blood as I could I saw that it was a male kestrel. These are super birds, with a facility for defying the laws of gravity and apparently standing still in mid-air that never ceases to amaze me. One of my greatest joys it to watch them skimming through the skies, hovering over their prey and then swooping in for the kill. Sadly this hovering makes them very easy prey for the kind of nut who shoots anything that moves, plus quite a few things that don't. As their 'sportsmanship' usually stops short of checking that their victims are decently dead, all too often wounded kestrels face a slow and painful end. I wasn't too optimistic about this one's chances of survival; if his injuries didn't kill him the shock probably would. And once a wild bird makes up its mind to die there's very little anyone can do to save it. All I could do was treat him for shock and make sure that if he did die at least he'd die in comfort. There was

15

no point in worrying about his injuries at this stage; if they were really severe he wouldn't survive anyway, and if they were relatively minor they could wait until he was over the shock. The immediate requirements were warmth, quiet and darkness. One of my more inspired auction buys was a heated Hostess tray, but as I tend to be something of a hit-and-miss hostess it had never so far figured in my entertaining, and the chances were it never would. But it made a marvellous bed-warmer for sick birds, I tucked the kestrel into a hay-lined box, placed the box – supported by a couple of bricks – on top of the tray and put the whole caboodle into a cupboard in the study. Now all I could do was wait and hope.

When I opened the cupboard next morning I was overjoyed to see that the kestrel was not only alive but looking quite perky. He hopped onto the edge of the box, fixing me with a basilisk stare, and I promptly dubbed him Basil. 'I see you've decided to live then,' I said conversationally, 'now let's see about treating your injuries.' One look at his wing, hanging uselessly and encrusted with blood (quite a bit of it Alec's, I shouldn't wonder – kestrels don't have those sharp talons and predatory beak for nothing) and I could see that this was a job for a professional. Tucking him back into his box, much to his disgust, I took him off to the vet.

Once the blood was cleaned off we could see the full extent of Basil's injuries. The pellet had gone right through the wing, damaging it badly, and Mr Partridge thought it unlikely that it would ever heal properly. This was bad news indeed. Even for a completely fit bird the battle for survival is pretty grim; a disabled bird would stand no chance at all. 'Poor Basil,' I commiserated. 'It looks as though we're stuck with one another.' He cocked a button-bright eye at me and I

16

thought I saw a gleam of horror. 'Still, look on the bright side,' I went on. 'Now that we know that you won't ever be strong enough to go free we don't have to worry about you getting too close to The Enemy. We can be friends!' This time there was no mistaking the look of horror in his eyes. Of course I didn't think for one moment that we would ever be friends, but knowing that he would never again have to take his chances in the world outside I could at least try to establish some sort of relationship with him – something I would never do with a bird that was to be released eventually. Life is tough enough for birds in the wild; if they lost their instinctive fear of humans they wouldn't stand a chance.

I fixed Basil up with a perch by the inglenook, well out of reach of the cats. Not that I anticipated any trouble from them, bravery not being their strong point. They took one look at Basil's predatory beak and unanimously decided that they had urgent business elsewhere. Thereafter they completely ignored him. To my surprise Basil took to domestic life as though he'd never known any other and very soon emerged as something of a character. The great love of his life was television; he found it absolutely enthralling and would sit entranced through the most utter rubbish, head nodding enthusiastically in unison with the characters. He was totally undiscriminating – with one exception. He couldn't stand football. Immediately a football programme came on he fluttered down from his perch, tripped purposefully over to the set and, screeching shrilly, systematically pecked all the players to death. As I myself find football only slightly less boring than watching paint dry I had to admire his taste.

Although Basil couldn't fly he could flutter about a bit and he soon came to terms with his limitations. He never made a move without plotting his route right down to the last detail. I could tell, just by watching his head movements, where he was planning to go and how he proposed to get there. Route worked out, he was now ready for the off. Perch to sofa, nod, nod (every move was accompanied by vigorous head-nodding) sofa to sideboard, nod, nod, sideboard to table nod, nod, table to windowsill – and who's a clever boy, then? Flushed with success he surveyed the room then immediately started planning his return journey: windowsill to table, table to sideboard, sideboard to sofa, sofa to – oh, hell! He looks up at his perch, way above his head, then beseechingly at me, then back to the perch again. I think he is trying to tell me something. I put out my hand and he hops onto my wrist and from there to his perch. Three brisk nods to show his appreciation, then he sets to work preening himself. Ten minutes later, every feather groomed to perfection, he is ready to repeat his grand tour. This goes on all evening and if by chance I am not at hand when he needs a leg-up he just sits on the sofa and screams till I come. At first I always wore gloves when handling him but I soon realised that it wasn't necessary. He would sit on my wrist, talons gripping just enough to give him a firm hold but never so strongly as to be uncomfortable.

One problem that had to be faced early on was feeding. Birds of prey must have fur or feather in their diet in order to digest their food. In the wild they get all the roughage they need from the mice, voles and other rodents and birds they prey on. But the living room is not exactly what you might call the natural habitat of these creatures so the pickings were a bit on the sparse side. It was no good looking to the cats to provide a regular supply of kestrel fodder; Flossie was the only hunter and she made darned sure that whatever she

18

caught she kept. So, with apologies to Mother Nature, I started creating my own little beasts. Feathers gleaned from the chickens and ducks and wrapped around a strip of beef transformed it into a bird that would have had Percy Edwards looking to his laurels. But, if I say it myself, my chef d'ouevre was my Mock Mouse (or Mousse). This was a chunk of beef lovingly moulded into a mouse shape and garnished with donkey combings. A few of donkey Simon's long shaggy hairs twisted into a reasonable facsimile of a tail added the finishing touch.

Basil eyed these offerings moodily for a moment or two before picking one up and inspecting it closely from every angle. He then fixed me with a long, meaningful stare which said clearly, 'This is not a mouse. You know it's not a mouse and I know it's not a mouse'. 'OK,' I snapped, 'So it's not a mouse. But it's still food. In fact it's even better than a mouse – it's got no bones.' He gave me to understand that this was not the point at issue; he was quite well aware that the misshapen mess he was clutching was food, and indeed had every intention of eating it in his own good time. Just so long as I didn't think I had put one over on him. After that I didn't bother about tarting up his food to look like the real thing. I just fed him amorphous blobs of meat wrapped in feathers and fur and Basil, honour satisfied, tore into them with enthusiasm. I was sad, in a way. Having discovered an unsuspected streak of creativity in my make-up it seemed a pity to have it crushed at birth.

As birds of prey hadn't figured large in my life up till then my knowledge about them was woefully sparse. I read all the available literature about kestrels but as it related exclusively to their life in the wild it wasn't very helpful. What I needed to know was how to care for

19

these birds in the home. So off I strolled to a bird sanctuary about twelve miles away for some first-hand advice. I got the advice, all right; I also got a cardboard box containing a sick gull. Gilbert, as I called him, was suffering from botulism, something to which gulls are particularly prone. He was well on the way to recovery but needed convalescent care prior to release. As he would be going back to the wild soon he couldn't be a house guest so I bedded him down in the barn and, except for feeding and changing his bedding, left him strictly alone. This was no great hardship as he wasn't an easy bird to love. He held me personally responsible for all his troubles and, not having much else to occupy his days, spent his time thinking up ways of getting back at me. He would lie in wait until I brought in his food then swoop down and make a grab for my hand. He would eat pretty well anything but given the choice he opted for my fingers every time. Fish fingers I could understand, but people fingers . . .? He was with me for ten fraught days and when he started flying at my face I thought, 'Right my lad. If you're fit enough for this sort of nonsense, you're fit enough to go.' Early next morning I gave him an enormous breakfast to set him up for the day, opened the barn door and stood back – only just in time. He whizzed past me, wings fanning my face and, without a backward glance let alone a word of thanks, soared over the hedge and was lost to view. I watched with mixed feelings: delight at his recovery, relief that my torn fingers would take no more punishment and concern about his future well-being. And I was surprised that I missed him, in a masochistic sort of way.

Meanwhile Basil was settling in very well and integrating nicely into the household. With compromises on both sides an acceptable life style was beginning to evolve – one that gave him maximum freedom and independence and me minimum aggro. The only thing we didn't see eye to eye on was the question of bedtime. I felt that he should go to bed at dusk, as he would in the wild. Basil disagreed; he considered that as he now led a domestic life he should go to bed at a domestic time, i.e. when the telly closed down. Every night we went through the same pantomime. 'Come on Basil, time for bed.' A look of horror spreads over his face and, forgetting his limitations, he takes off from his perch, dropping to the floor like a sack of potatoes. Lacking a public school education, I've never let the 'fair-play' ethic get in the way of achieving my ends, so I have no compunction about taking advantage of his weak position – I make a grab for him. He out-manoeuvres me, legs it to the window and scrambles up the curtains. Perched on top of the curtain pole he shrieks obsceni-ties at me. I reach up to grab him – he runs crabwise to the far end of the pole. We spend the next five minutes chasing from one end of the pole to the other until he decides he's had enough. He hops onto my shoulder – OK we've had our little frolic, let's go. Completely frazzled I carry him upstairs and as soon as I open the study door he jumps down, scuttles over to the open cage and hops in. Another bedtime over.

Of course I had no illusions that Basil's behaviour and temperament were typical of kestrels generally. One thing I've learned from the birds and animals that have come my way is that they are individuals. Basil just happened to be more individual than most – a 'one-off', just as Pooh, my much-loved and sadly missed ferret had been. If I had needed proof of Pooh's one-offness I had it in full measure a few weeks after his demise. Two young lads turned up on my doorstep clutching a battered wooden box. 'We heard your ferret died so we've brought you another one.' My heart sank. I didn't want another ferret because I knew the chances of finding two Poohs in one lifetime were virtually nil. The newcomer would have to be treated like a proper ferret, kept away from the chickens and ducklings and probably shut up in a cage for the rest of its life. I hate the idea of keeping any fit, healthy creature permanently caged. On the other hand, I couldn't throw this generous, thoughtful gesture back in these youngsters' faces. 'That's very kind of you,' I said, taking the box from them. 'Thank you very much indeed.' 'That'll be two quid,' said the older of the two '£1.50 for the ferret and 50 pence for the box.' You crafty little buggers, I thought, scrabbling through my purse for the money. Not only do you land me with a flipping incubus, you charge me £2 for the privilege.

I lined a converted sideboard with hay, put in food and water and, after donning a pair of thick gloves, took the ferret out of his box. The gloves turned out to be entirely cosmetic; shooting me a look of pure venom he sank his teeth into my thumb and just hung on. Blood soaked through the glove and, without loosening his grip, he started licking it. Ye gods, I thought, I've got a bloody man-eater. Grabbing his tail with my free hand I yanked at it till he let go, then dropped him unceremoniously into his new home. I went inside and nursed my sore thumb, seething with fury at those two snotty-nosed kids for putting one over on me and at myself for letting them. By the next day I had cooled off enough to consider the situation rationally. I wasn't being fair to the ferret; he was in a strange environment being handled by someone he didn't know and therefore, had no reason to trust. In the circumstances his behaviour was entirely normal – for a normal ferret. It was unrealistic to compare him with Pooh who had

22

been anything but normal, ferret-wise. Given time and care he would learn, if not to love me, at least to trust me. Of course he would never be another Pooh but this was hardly his fault.

Awash with penitence and head whirling with high-minded resolutions I went outside to make my peace with the newcomer. One look at the empty cage and the freshly gnawed hole in the side and I realised that my newcomer was now a new-goner. With a sense of impending doom I rushed off to check on the birds. The two broody hens were lying dead in their pens, their eggs scattered and broken. The other chickens and Henrietta the hybrid fowl were sitting in a frozen row on a branch of the apple tree, paralysed with fright. A muffled quacking led me to the barn, where the ducks were huddled together in a corner, swapping horror stories. But where were Gussie and Griselda, my doughty guard geese? And why hadn't they seen the assassin off? Good heavens, if they could put the fear of God into me surely they should have had no difficulty frightening off a ferret? I eventually found them, cowering with fear, in a corner of the donkey shelter. Standing protectively over them wwas my lovely gentle Simon. I called to the geese and they came creeping out, looking sheepish and cowed as I had never seen them before. It didn't last, of course. One look at me and they decided that it was all my fault (the bad things that happen always are; the good things are taken completely for granted). Stretching their necks and hissing like a barrelful of vipers, they charged. Caught unawares I lost my balance and fell flat on my face. Simon, bless him, came over and stood between me and the geese who, deprived of their fun, scuttled off across the paddock chittering with frustration. Grabbing Simon's neck I hauled myself up off the ground and did a bit of chittering myself. The other three donkeys were standing in a semi-circle eyeing me with interest; Phil and Sophie looked concerned but Humphrey made no attempt to hide the fact that he had found the whole business enormously amusing. His eyes glowed with humour: Gosh, that was funny! Do it again! I snarled at him and was immediately overcome with shame. 'Where's your sense of humour?' I asked myself. 'I'll look for it later', I replied. 'Right now I've got to find a fugitive ferret before he wipes out the rest of my livestock.' I didn't have far to look; the ferret was back in his cage, busily washing the blood off his self-satisfied face. After plugging up the hole and putting a brick against it just in case, I went inside to make a phone call. Twenty minutes later Reg the Rabbiter arrived and I bade farewell to the ferret with a gladsome heart.

So I had no illusions that any future kestrels that might come my way would be anything like Basil, and I was quite right. I have lost count of the number of kestrels I have cared for and although they were all different in temperament, there was never another Basil. Which was just as well because most of them are returned to the wild eventually. Two who became permanent residents were Sid and Liz. Liz was very badly hurt and had to have a wing amputated so her future here is assured. Sid's injuries were relatively minor and he was fit to go in a matter of weeks. But would he go? Would he hell! I gave him a hearty breakfast, opened the door of their enclosure and said, 'Off you go.' He cocked a beady eye, snuggled closer to Liz and said, 'Who, me? No fear.' 'Now don't be ridiculous,' 'I protested, 'I can't keep you here, there's nothing wrong with you.' 'I'm not shifting', said he. 'You want me out, you'll have to throw me out.' I didn't

flatter myself that Sid's reluctance to leave had anything to do with me, it was his devotion to Liz that kept him here. I knew that Liz would miss him dreadfully but was that a good enough reason to keep a perfectly fit bird in captivity? In any case there would be other injured kestrels coming along to keep her company. Still, I felt very mean and tried not to catch her eye when I went into the enclosure and grabbed a highly indignant Sid. 'Now just stop this nonsense,' I told him. 'You've got the whole wide world out there – trees and woods and voles and field-mice. You can't possibly want to spend the rest of your life in captivity. Your devotion to Liz does you great credit but the world is full of lady kestrels.' He looked shocked and gave me to understand that promiscuity might be all right for people but, speaking for himself, he was a one-gal guy.

25

'We'll see,' I said and taking him over to the far field, which is a favourite hunting ground for kestrels, tossed him gently into the air. He circled twice and soared off towards the woods.

Relieved that his release had passed off without undue trauma I went back to make my peace with Liz. Sitting on top of the enclosure, shrieking his head off, was an exceedingly disgruntled Sid. 'What kept you?' he screeched. 'I've been waiting ages. Get that door open.' Which I did, and in he flew. Bustling over to Liz, who welcomed him with open wings – or, more accurately, wing – he told her all about his short-lived adventure in shrill piercing tones. Liz listened intently, nodding her head sympathetically from time to time.

After two or three more fruitless efforts to release Sid I gave up, figuring that he probably knew best. From time to time I leave the enclosure door open and offer him his freedom, just in case he's changed his mind; sometimes he comes out and flutters to the top of the enclosure, where he spends about five minutes chittering to an awe-struck Liz before flying in again. More often he just sits looking from the open door to me and then back at the door again as if to say, 'I don't wish to tell you your business, but you do know that you've left the door open?'

Temperamentally, Sid and Liz are poles apart. Liz is a very gentle sweet-natured lady who takes things as they come, accepting her disability philosophically. Sid, on the other hand, is pure macho, strutting belligerently up and down his perch and screaming obscenities at any stranger rash enough to come within yelling distance. When I take in their food he goes wild with excitement, bounding up and down on his perch and nodding joyously. I always feed Liz first but she never takes a bit until Sid has inspected both their meals and decided which one he wants. Sometimes he decides that he wants them both and Liz, never having heard of Women's Lib (Kestrel Division) sits quietly by and lets him get on with it. At first I was incensed at this appalling behaviour until I discovered that Sid was stockpiling food in a secret cache and, when he thought nobody was looking, would bring out selected titbits and feed them to Liz.

As the numbers of prey birds swelled, so the problems of feeding them increased. It was all very well wrapping bits of meat in fur and feather when I only had Basil to cater for, but on a large scale it was quite impracticable. Apart from the time involved in furring and feathering every mouthful of food, there were only so many feathers and donkey combings available.  Ever since the first donkey arrived there has been an unwritten agreement with the wild birds that they have first pickings of the combings. Come spring and I shouldn't think there is a nest in the vicinity that isn't lined with donkey hair. So they were most put out when I started collecting the combings to provide roughage for the prey birds. 'Thief,' they twittered. 'Nest robber! Baby basher!' I felt awful. And I found that I couldn't pass a chicken without eyeing it speculatively, looking for a feather that seemed a bit on the loose side. The chickens, for their part, began to get a haunted look, metaphorically clutching their feathers to their bosoms and screaming 'rape' every time I hove into view. So when I heard that a local hatchery had supplies of frozen day-old chicks this seemed to be the answer to my problems. Well, to one of them. There was still the problem of coming to terms with actually feeding these chicks to my non-paying guests. What sort of monster was I, drooling sentimentally over my own fluffy little chicklets while at the same time feeding their less

27

fortunate brethren to the birds of prey? I sat down and thought about it objectively; these hatchery chicks were dead anyway and whether or not I fed them to the other birds nothing was going to change that. At least, by providing a meal for the birds of prey, they were forging an important link in the food chain. I wasn't entirely convinced – my head knew it made sense, but the rest of me was sickened by the whole business. To this day I find I can't look those pathetic little chicks in the frozen eye.

People say to me, 'I suppose you're a vegetarian', and look surprised when I tell them I'm not. I can understand this – my own feeling is that I should be vegetarian. But I would still have to feed meat and fish to the carnivores and prey birds, so what would be the point? Although I have noticed that my eating habits are being affected by the animals and birds themselves. Chicken is out – I can't look at a chicken drumstick without conjuring up a picture of one of the resident hens hobbling about on one leg. Roast duck is instantly translated into roast Quaggy and lamb chops into chubby-chops Jason, with a consequent loss of appetite for either. And though I can't pretend that there was any love lost between Percy and me, I still can't bring myself to eat guinea fowl.

I know that scientists insist that animals have no 'feelings', at least not in the way that people have, and they may very well be right. But until these experts come up with some definite proof I'll go right on assuming that animals and birds, in their own way, feel grief, joy, anger, fear, love and any number of other so-called human emotions. This is not to say that some of us animal nuts don't occasionally go to extremes in our anxiety not to offend our pets; suffering cramp rather than hurt the cat's feelings by pushing him off our lap; apologising profusely when we accidently trip over him; saying 'thank you' when he proudly brings us a mouse; when all our instincts are to shriek, 'take that disgusting thing outside!'

When I was living in the caravan a friend gave me a tatty old goatskin rug that she was on the point of throwing away. Not being one to let pride stand in the way of something-for-nothing, and overcoming my principles about the obscenity of using animal skins in this way by rationalising that I wouldn't be saving the life of a single goat by refusing the offer, I took it. But when Barney the goat joined the household I was disgusted and sickened by the sight of the rug; for all I knew, it could have been Barney's mum. Terrified that he might catch sight of it and be traumatised for life I wrapped it up and put it into a plastic sack preparatory to taking it to the dump. Five minuters later I was shattered to see that Barney had ripped the sack apart and was happily making a meal of the rug.

CHAPTER 3

I woke up to a white world and realised that the snows had come again. And with the snows came the inevitable drifts along the path, cutting me off from the world outside. Still, this was my third winter in the country and I'd learned a thing or two. The freezers and barn were packed solid with food and for the first time I was cosily ensconced in my lovely warm cottage. 'Let it snow,' I carolled selfishly. 'Who cares?' Actually, I did. The more comfortable I was, the more I worried about the creatures struggling to survive in the frozen wasteland. The wild birds were all right; I had set up a cafeteria service along the lines of the Windmill (We Never Close) and thanks to a friendly neighbourhood baker who let me have all his unsold bread, plus peanuts filched from the resident birds and corn filched from the donkeys, there was a plentiful supply of food for them. It was the non-hibernating mammals I was worried about.

Feeding the donkeys early one morning I noticed fox tracks criss-crossing the snow-covered paddock. As I was following them to their source I had an uncanny feeling that I was being watched. The snow muffled all sound and the intense silence added to the general eeriness. I looked around and caught a movement under the hedge; feeling the hairs prickle at the back of my neck I crept slowly towards it. There, huddled under a bush, was a grey vixen. Thin, gaunt and shivering she made no attempt to flee when she saw me. I was shocked at her condition – she looked as though she hadn't eaten for weeks. And, of course, the weaker she became through hunger the less able she was to hunt for food. It was a vicious circle.

I rushed back to the barn and raided the animals' freezer for liver. But it would take ages to thaw, even if I put it in boiling water, and there wasn't that much time. I opened a couple of tins of cat food – the cats don't eat tinned food but I like to keep a supply just in case – and hurried back to the paddock. The vixen was still there and, getting as close as I dared without frightening her, I tipped the two tins out onto the ground. Her nose twitched and she staggered shakily to her feet; half a dozen quick gulps and the food was gone. With a sigh of what I like to think was satisfaction she crept back under the hedge and collapsed in a heap. Back to the cottage where I fussed and fumed over the liver, willing it to thaw. 'Hurry up, hurry up,' I muttered impatiently. 'Yes, hurry up,' echoed the cats who were sitting in a hopeful semi-circle at my feet, convinced that the liver was for them. 'Don't push your luck,' I warned them, 'You've already had your breakfast.' 'Yes, we know,' they chorused, 'but we're the only ones who eat liver so it must be for us.' 'That's what you think,' I said.

I cut the liver into manageable chunks, as the vixen didn't look as though she had the strength to cope with anything too large, and took it out to her. One by one I threw the pieces to her and watched as she gulped them down. The last two pieces she buried in the snow – obviously her hunger was satisfied. I fed her again in the

evening and was pleased to see that, although she ate
with relish, she wasn't wolfing (or should it be foxing?)
the food down as ravenously as she had earlier. The
next morning she was gone; I followed her tracks and
when I was about ten feet from the edge of the woods a
shadowy figure emerged from behind a tree and stood
watching me. 'She looks better already,' I thought,
with more hope than truth. In fact she looked pretty
dreadful, but at least she was on her feet. 'Room
service,' I announced, tossing the meat to her. Again
she ate her fill but this time, insteady of burying the
surplus food, she disappeared into the woods with it.
That evening she was waiting for me when I brought
her supper, and again at breakfast time next morning.
This went on for three days – on the fourth day she
didn't come. I left her food in the usual place and when

I went back later it had gone, but of course there was no way of telling whether she had eaten it, or some other animal. I continued leaving out food for her but I never saw her again. Either help had come too late to save her or her weakened state had made her an easy target for the farmer's gun.

Now that I'd established the practice of leaving food in the paddock every day I had to go on doing it, otherwise whatever creature had been eating it might well grab a chicken or duck in lieu. So every evening, just before dusk, I put out meat and scraps and waited by the paddock gate to see what happened. For the first four days nothing did, unless you count chilblains, frostbite and a streaming cold, although the food was always gone by the morning. Then on the fifth day I spotted a fox creeping cautiously across the adjoining field; every few minutes he stopped and sniffed the air before moving on again. He didn't make directly for the meat but approached it by a sort of zig-zag route. One last look round, then a swift grab and he was off into the woods with his haul. About ten minutes later he was back for seconds – and then thirds. Just as he was making off with the last piece a second fox emerged from the opposite field and picked his way warily over to the now depleted food depot. Thwarted, he stood sniffing the ground for a moment or two before slouching off towards the woods. After that I started scattering the meat around the paddock instead of leaving it all in one place and within about ten days I had a regular clientele of 5 free-loaders. There was an enormous pale yellow dog fox who looked exactly like a lion, a smaller dark brown one and two red and white vixens. But my favourite was a little frisky gold and white chap who was invariably the first to arrive and the last to leave and so always got the pick of the food.

After a while the foxes became more daring and I no longer had to hide while they were eating. Shooting me a cautious glance to let me know that they knew I was there, they made a bee-line for the food, grabbed it in their jaws and made off with it. But none of them came as close as little Crazy (Like a Fox). Each night I left the food a little closer to my viewing post, to see how near he would venture, and each night he trotted over to get it until he came close enough for me to touch him. I didn't, of course! But I was warmed by his trust. My greatest fear was that my neighbours would find out that I was running a soup kitchen for indigent foxes. Really, I told myself, they should be grateful to me. Well-fed foxes don't raid chicken runs, so actually I'm doing them a favour. But I doubt if they would have seen it that way.

This was the domestic birds' first winter and I was a bit worried about how they'd cope with snow and frost. The ducks and chickens took it in their stride but Gussie and Griselda were most put out. Nothing gives them greater pleasure than having something to gripe about and they found plenty that winter. Every time I went outside I had to listen to a catalogue of complaints delivered in a querulous, high-pitched, squawking monotone: the pond has gone all hard and funny, how are we supposed to swim in it? And all this white stuff hurts our toes and is giving us chilblains. And we can't sit down because we'll get a cold in our kidneys. We're very unhappy and it's all your fault. Well, there was nothing new about that. Nobody cares about my chilblains and kidneys, I thought sullenly as I got the pickaxe and started breaking up the ice on the pond, closely watched by a pair of highly critical geese. I was doing it all wrong; I was too slow; I was churning up the mud under the ice; why had I started this side of the pond when I knew perfectly well that they always launched themselves from the other side . . . ? 'Oh, shut up!' I snapped, thoroughly riled by now. The next thing I knew there was an excruciating pain in my rear, my legs took on a life of their own and I shot head-first across the ice. Gibbering with rage I clutched my throbbing rump and screamed, 'Who did that? Who bit me?' Gussie and Griselda were standing by the side of the pond, watching my antics with undisguised delight and nodding approvingly. I looked longingly at the pickaxe and was shocked to discover that I had homicidal tendencies. I don't really think I would have parted their feathers with it, but for a split second I was very, very tempted! Well, there's one good thing about it, I consoled myself – for the first time since the snows came, Gussie and Griselda actually look happy!

A few weeks later tragedy struck. Griselda, who just couldn't keep her beak out of anything, got her head stuck in the donkeys' haynet. The more she struggled the more entwined she became. Alerted by Gussie's hysterical screeching I rushed over, but I could see from her limp body that it was already too late. Gussy was in a frenzy, running around in circles and screaming his head off. As soon as he saw me he ran over to stand in front of Griselda; neck outstretched and wings spread, he dared me to go near her. And there he stayed all day, keeping his sad, lonely and exceedingly vocal vigil. It wasn't till evening, when I managed to entice him into the enclosure, that I was able to disentangle Griselda and give her a decent burial.

Over the following days my heart bled for Gussie; he and Griselda had been so much of a unit that it was as though he had lost a part of himself. All day he sat at the spot where she'd met her end, just waiting. Every time one of the ducks ventured near he would look up

35

hopefully then, seeing that it wasn't Griselda, sink back into his torpor. From time to time he left his post and wandered dispiritedly around, calling and calling to her. He lost all interest in food and, equally alarming, he lost all interest in attacking me. This was really serious. The obvious solution was to get him another mate, except that I wasn't too sure whether this would be a solution. Some water fowl mate for life, frequently going into a decline when their mates die and ultimately joining them in that great goose house in the Sky. I couldn't let this happen to such a spirited creature as Gussy. Besides, I missed our daily skirmishes; the only exercise I got was galloping around the garden with a snapping beak about three inches away from my fast-retreating backside. And in any case he was much too young for permanent widower-hood.

Mind made up, I went over to Gussie to put him in the picture. He looked up dully as I approached and I found myself almost willing him to attack me, but it was no go. He gave an enormous sigh and turned away. It tore me apart to see the change in him but I felt that a show of sympathy at this stage would be counter-productive; he needed to be snapped out of his misery. Briskly I informed him that his fortunes were about to take an upward swing. His devotion to Griselda's memory did him great credit but life must go on. To this end a marriage was about to be arranged, so would he kindly perk himself up a bit, give his sadly-neglected feathers a once-over-lightly and prepare to meet his bride.

It wasn't until I was back in the cottage that it occurred to me that I had been a bit hasty, glibly making promises to Gussie when I didn't even know whether I'd be able to find a mate for him. If past experience was anything to go by the chances were that my search would produce a plethora of promises, hordes of stories about the goose that got away, heart-felt regrets that I hadn't come last week when they had 37 lady geese seeking a good home, and totally fictitious addresses of non-existent people who they knew for sure had a goose for sale. The one thing it would not produce would be a real, live, honest-to-goodness goose. With very little hope I rang Mr Newbury and told him all my troubles. 'Do you want a gosling or a fully grown goose?' he asked. 'Oh, a fully grown one,' I said. I couldn't trust Gussie with a gosling and the situation was too desperate to wait for a little one to grow up – by that time I doubted whether Gussie would still be with us. In that case, said he, my troubles were over. He had just the thing, a beautiful 18-month-old . . . 'She'll do,' I interrupted excitedly. 'I'm on my way,' and I dashed out to the car. 'And this time,' I vowed, 'I'll make darned sure that his smart-alec jay doesn't make a monkey out of me.'

I drove into the yard and got out of the car then, before the jay had a chance to stick his oar in I announced in clear ringing tones that Mr Newbury was expecting me, he knew I was coming and therefore would be waiting for me. So there was absolutely no point in telling me he was out. In the resounding silence that followed this speech I became aware that I was not alone. I looked round and there was Mr Newbury leaning on the gate regarding me with interest. 'If you're talking to Jacey,' he observed, 'you're wasting your breath. He's round the back pulling all the pegs off the washing line.' And no doubt laughing his beak off at making a fool of me yet again, I reflected sourly.

Mr Newbury introduced me to Gussie's prospective bride and my immediate, quite unworthy reaction was, 'She's much too good for him.' Because she really was

37

an absolute charmer. Having become accustomed to living with geese whose features were not designed to register any expression other than distaste, displeasure or downright malice, I found Suzie's sweet benign face utterly devastating. Her frilly feathers were white with golden brown tips and they curled all around her legs and body, reaching almost to the ground and giving the impression that she was wearing a petticoat. 'She's a Sebastopol,' Mr Newbury told me. 'They all have curly feathers.' 'She can be up-the-pole for all I care,' I replied. 'She's stunning'. Just then an elderly grey goose emerged from the barn and waddled stiffly towards us. Her flaccid undercarriage all but scraped the ground as she very slowly picked her way over to Suzie, who greeted her with a soft whimper and a gentle nuzzle.

It turned out that the geriatric goose had belonged to some neighbours who were planning to kill her now that her egg-laying days were over. Feeling that this was an unseemly end for such an amiable old biddy Mr Newbury had taken her in so that she could enjoy her remaining years in a happy, unthreatening atmosphere. I was immensely moved by this. 'Really,' I told him, 'you should be ashamed. A hard-headed commercial breeder like you taking in pensioners! You're just an old softie!' He looked abashed. 'I know,' he said, 'that's why I'll never be rich.' Join the club, I thought. He went on to add that the old lady earned her keep by mothering all the orphaned babies; she was particularly attached to Suzie as she had brought her up from a tot. I looked up at him sharply; was he trying to say something without actually saying it? They would miss each other terribly, he went on. This time I was sure – he was trying to tell me something. As casually as I knew how I mumbled something about tragic to break them up, never know what effect it might have on them, don't suppose he'd let me have them both, too much to ask, of course . . . His face brightened. 'I was hoping you'd offer. I know she'd pine if she was left here on her own. I'll get a box.' Well, well Gussie, I mused, two wives for the price of one. You are a lucky chap.

On the journey home I fretted and worried, as I always do, about whether I'd done the right thing, mentally listing all the possible things that could go wrong, plus quite a few improbable ones. The biggest worry was that Gussie would resent Suzie and Esme and attack them. The second biggest was that he and Suzie would take to each other and leave poor Esme out in the cold. The third . . . oh, this was becoming too ridiculous for words!

Faithful Gussie was still keeping his lonely vigil when we arrived home. I set the box down by the side of the pond, opened it and then stood back to await developments. They weren't long in coming; the ducks and chickens immediately came charging over to see what was going on. Gussie for his part didn't even bother to look up. After a moment or two Suzie eased herself out of the box and looked all around her. A few seconds later she was joined by Esme. The pair of them stood still for a moment or two and then Suzie spotted Gussie. With a honk of delight she went careering over to him, with Esme trundling creakily in her wake and me no less creakily, and somewhat apprehensively, bringing up the rear. I picked up a stick, just in case hostilities broke out. Suzie, to my mind displaying courage of a very high order, trotted straight up to Gussie and in a soft, chuckling voice started to tell him the story of her life. Esme stood on the sideline interjecting the odd comment from time to time. After the first hopeful

glance Gussie looked away and resumed his study of the horizon. Not in the least deterred Suzie continued her monologue without pausing for breath and, as far as I could make out, not once repeating herself. How long this might have gone on heaven only knows, but after about five minutes Quaggy the mallard drake suddenly appeared on the scene. By now he was over his fixation for me and was showing a healthy interest in the feathered sorority. Unfortunately, his early attachment to a human bird had affected his perception of the non-human variety; he was only interested in big birds – the bigger the better. As he himself is very small, even for a mallard, this presented certain difficulties when it came to mating. He found it almost impossible to mount his chosen one and when he did manage it he usually fell off before he could make any impression on her. Sometimes his swain wasn't even aware of his attentions and would waddle off with a fiercely resolute Quaggy hanging on like grim death.

A lesser drake would have accepted his limitations and settled for what he could get, but not Quaggy. On the contrary, he was determined to go on to bigger and better things – and what could be bigger than a goose? I had caught him from time to time eyeing Griselda speculatively and even, on a couple of occasions when presumably his ardour overcame his instinct for self-preservation, trying it on with her. He never got to first base, Gussy saw to that, but he wasn't easily deterred. So when he spotted Suzie, a vision of loveliness if ever there was one, and big with it, he couldn't believe his luck. Quacking happily he bustled over to her, flapped up onto her back and grabbed the back of her head in his bill. Taken completely by surprise Suzie stopped abruptly in mid-sentence and looked around sharply to see who was taking outrageous liberties with her. The

next second all hell broke loose; with a squawk of rage
Gussie shot to his feet and made a grab for Quaggy.
Quaggy lost his grip, slid off Suzie's back and was
almost trampled to death by Esme. Fearing for Quaggy's safety I charged in brandishing my stick and beat
Gussy off – rather bravely, now I come to think of it – all
the while yelling to Quaggy to run for his life while he
had the chance. But Quaggy had apparently decided
that death was preferable to dishonour and, quacking
hysterically, hurled himself at Gussie. I grabbed him
just in time and hauled him off before Gussie did him
a serious mischief. Quaggy was furious. 'I could have
handled him,' he hoinked, 'he was beginning to
weaken. A quick jab to the jaw and another to the head
and I'd have finished him off.' 'Yes, I know,' I soothed
him. 'You're a gutsy little chap and I'm proud of you.' I
set him down at a safe distance and went back to see
what was going on in the goose community. To my joy
Gussie was strutting proudly around his domain, Suzie
on one side and Esme on the other. Well done, Quaggy,
I thought – at least you've jolted Gussie out of his
slough. Though I doubted if Quaggy would regard this
as an achievement to gladden the heart.

CHAPTER 4

On the domestic front things were settling down very nicely. Now that the cats had decided to live in the cottage and were making their muddy-pawed mark on the carpets and upholstery it was beginning to take on a comfortable, homely (well, all right, scruffy) look that was very much to my liking. Already the memories of roughing it in the caravan were beginning to fade and I was taking luxuries like hot water, lights at the touch of a switch and central heating entirely for granted. Sitting by the fire one night covered in cats I was suddenly jolted out of my mood of utter contentment by an odd clicking noise. The cats heard it too and immediately snapped to attention, noses quivering and whiskers twitching. Dear God, I thought, death watch beetle! Tuning in to the cats' antennae I traced the sound to the fireplace and couldn't believe my luck – a cricket on the hearth! How's that for a cliche, I thought.

I can't pretend that everything about the cottage was perfect. As time wore on so my list of things-I-would-do-differently-if-I-had-it-to-do-over lengthened. For all that my friends disapproved of my move to the country they were agreed on one thing: I was terribly lucky to have a house that was being virtually rebuilt from scratch. 'You'll be able to have it exactly the way you want it,' they enthused. 'Sockets where you need them, not where the builder thinks they ought to go. Light fittings in planned positions instead of stuck any old where. It's a marvellous opportunity to do it your way.' Yes, as long as you have some idea of what your way is and what your needs are going to be. Not being over-endowed with imagination I just couldn't translate the stark, empty expanses of space into rooms in which I would actually be living, cooking and sleeping. The one thing I was sure about was that I wanted lots and lots of power points. And I got them – all in places that I can't get to without performing athletic feats of Olympic proportions or moving half the furniture. And the light fittings are so positioned that they illuminate parts

of the room that nobody in their right mind would want illuminated, while vital parts are left in Stygian gloom. For example, in the kitchen the bin and draining board are brilliantly highlighted, but the cooker and sink are shrouded in shadows. And the wall lights in the bedroom cast their glow over the wardrobe while I peer myopically through the blurry haze at the book I am trying to read in bed. But, if I say it myself, the choice of position for the bathroom light displayed the kind of ineptitude that borders on genius. Even now I can't fathom the reasoning behind my decision to have it sited right bang over the bath. Fortunately the electrician agreed that it wasn't exactly the ideal position for a light fitting (although it would have been a darned sight more helpful if he'd said so before actually installing the light) and moved it to a safer spot. But he left the cable sticking out of the wall as a permanent reminder of my abject stupidity. Even on the rare occasions when I got the position right I somehow managed to get the choice of fitting wrong. The beautiful pendant, not-quite-antique light fitting I picked up at an auction was perfect for the hall – the first thing to catch visitors eyes when the door was opened. Unfortunately the impact turned out to be even more dramatic than I envisaged; the first time the door was opened it caught the light a hefty wallop and smashed it to smithereens.

Although auctions are marvellous for picking up things at a fraction of the price you would pay in a shop, there is one big snag, particularly for electrical or mechanical items – they almost never have the instruction booklet with them. The hob unit I bought was an absolute snip; brand new (it was part of the stock of a trader who had gone broke) and the last word in high technology. But I hadn't the faintest idea how it worked. I was used to a simple four-burner four-knob cooker – the control panel of this one, which was only marginally less complicated than the instrument panel of Concorde, completely defeated me. Even now, after several years, some of the dials and knobs are still a mystery to me. With the built-in oven, however, I did get lucky; it came complete with full instructions for operating, dismantling, cleaning, etc. But as they were all in Spanish they were hardly more helpful than no instructions at all.

But still the biggest problem was the water, or rather the water supply. (When I mentioned to my sister that I was having water trouble she said, in all seriousness 'It's your age, dear. Why don't you see a doctor?') The pressure, which has always been of the trickle rather than the cascade variety, was gradually getting lower and lower until it was taking anything up to an hour to fill one donkey bucket. When a Water Board official tried to measure the pressure he found it was too low even to register on his gauge. He explained that as the water supply to the cottage is piped from a neighbouring farm it is classified as a private supply and is therefore outside the jurisdiction of the water authority, so I had to call in an independent company. After turning on a few taps in the cottage and solemnly studying plans of the water system they diagnosed corrosion of the pipe connecting the cottage to the farm. The only solution was to dig up the old pipe and put in a new one and that will be £598 please, thank you very much. This was a real body blow – buying and converting the cottage and furnishing it, albeit with secondhand stuff, had taken every penny of my savings. I could no more lay my hands on £598 than I could on £598,000. There was nothing else for it, I would just have to learn to live with my trickle and pray it wouldn't eventually find the uphill struggle through the thrombosed pipe too much of a challenge and give up completely.

The next few weeks were too awful to think about, even now. The tap feeding the pipe to the donkeys' buckets had to be left permanently on because the donkeys emptied the buckets faster than they could be filled. This meant that there was no water anywhere else; if I wanted to use the loo or have a bath I had to turn off the supply to the donkeys well in advance so that the tank would have a chance to fill. The donkeys, of course, took great exception to this and showed their displeasure by tipping up their buckets and kicking them around the paddock. Perhaps it was just that I was now particularly water-conscious but it did seem to me that the donkeys were drinking far more than they usually did. I found myself hanging around their water buckets, monitoring every sip they took. 'You can't possibly want another drink, you've only just had one.' Four astonished faces, water dripping off their chins, looked at me. 'Drip into the buckets,' I screamed, 'Don't waste it on the ground!' What was particularly galling about the whole business was that, following the thaw, the garden, the paddock, every square inch around the cottage was completely waterlogged – there was water everywhere except where I needed it. Then I happened to run into Mr Sludge who was having a lovely wallow in the septic tank at a neighbouring farm. He waved a rubbery pink hand and called out 'Any trouble with your pit?/I'll come and have a look at it.' 'It's not my pit, it's my water,' I wailed, grateful for a sympathetic ear. 'The water isn't coming through, I simply don't know what to do.' God help us, I thought, he's got me doing it now! 'Tried your stopcock?' he asked helpfully. 'If you can't get water through/that

46

is what you oughta do.' The stopcock! I hadn't thought of that.

I raced back to the cottage and found the stopcock under the sink. After grappling with a wrench for about twenty minutes I finally managed to loosen it; taking a deep breath I very tentatively turned on the tap – and lo! There was water! Not a gush exactly, but certainly a vast improvement on the dribble I'd lived with for the past few weeks. Ecstatic, I galloped outside and filled all the donkey buckets to overflowing. 'Drink,' I enjoined them. 'Come fill the cup and lap it up.' (Really, I thought, I must stop seeing Mr Sludge.) The donkeys regarded me coolly: No thank you, we're not thirsty now. Once the initial wave of euphoria had subsided a little I considered the situation carefully and latched onto the one positive aspect of the whole miserable business – what a good job it was that I was penniless. If I had been flush to the tune of £598 I would have blued the lot on replacing a pipe that didn't need replacing. Oh, blessed are the poor, I chirruped happily. I had much to be happy about. What with the hassle of moving into the cottage and one thing and another the winter months had flown by and it was spring – my first spring in the cottage.

Soon after this I got a phone call from a local animal sanctuary – could I take in a donkey 'just for a few weeks' while they tried to find a permanent home for him? Where were you when I needed you? I thought wryly, remembering all the trouble I'd had trying to find a donkey companion for Humphrey. Now that he had a companion and his companion had companions and quite truthfully my donkey cup was pretty well overflowing along came people begging me to take in donkeys. 'Tell me more,' I said cautiously. I knew that I'd take the donkey anyway but I didn't want to give the

47

impression that I was a complete pushover. It turned out that he wasn't a 'rescued' donkey; he hadn't been neglected or ill-treated, it was just that his owners could no longer keep him and had asked the welfare society to find him a good home. So at least he wouldn't have any of the emotional hang-ups that Simon had suffered when he first came. Even so, he would need lots of care and love to help him over the trauma of leaving his family and home. I said yes, I would be happy to have him on the understanding that it *was* a temporary arrangement, as the paddock wasn't big enough to support five donkeys. 'Thank you very much,' they said, 'We'll bring him over tomorrow. By the way, his name is Sailor.' 'You must be joking,' I gasped. 'No way am I going to go around saying "Hallo Sailor" to a donkey. While he's here he'll be kown as Wailer.' As it turned out, my choice of name was infinitely more suitable.

I went outside and called a meeting of the resident donkeys. 'Your numbers are about to be swelled by the arrival of a newcomer called Wailer,' I informed them. 'As a guest he is to be accorded every courtesy and consideration. He will probably be feeling miserable when he arrives so it is up to all of us to make sure that he feels wanted and loved. Understood?' They assumed their butter-wouldn't-melt-in-our-mouths expressions and nodded soberly. They didn't fool me for a moment but it was worth a try.

So we were all prepared when Wailer arrived – in a horse-box yet! No tatty old trailer for him. What we weren't prepared for was Wailer himself. The ramp was let down and out tripped a high-stepping, sleek-coated, incredibly classy vision of donkey elegance. My mob stared in astonishment – I don't think they even recognised the fugitive from Horse and Hound as a donkey. Even Humphrey for once was stunned into inactivity. Wailer paused and looked around him. His gaze swept the paddock, immediately transmuting it in my eyes to a grotty backyard, and his aristocratic nose quivered fastidiously. He then turned his attention to the four ragamuffins who were regarding him with wide-eyed disbelief and, with a disdain that bespoke several hundred years of selective breeding, curled his lip. He saved me for last – a shrewd move, this. Having witnessed his devastating dimissal of the in-house donkeys and his profound contempt for his surroundings, I was now completely demoralised. I was painfully conscious of the fact that my sweater had seen better days, there was a hole in the knee of my jeans and I was wearing odd wellies.

Aware that he had established a pyschological advantage, Wailer gave me a withering glance and then with studied insolence turned his back on me. Feeling about three inches tall, I looked up and caught Humphrey's eye. There was a gleam in it that, roughly translated, read, 'Don't worry, I know how to handle snooty upstarts. I'll soon cut him down to size.' Yes, I know, I thought – that's what I'm worried about. Poor Wailer had already been through enough, what with losing his home and finally landing up in what, by his standards, must have looked like Skid Row; the last thing he needed was a confrontation with a bunch of hoodlums. On the other hand if he was to become a member of the coterie, albeit on a temporary basis, the sooner his position was established the better. I knew Humphrey well enough not be too worried about Wailer's welfare; there is no malice in Humphrey, just an over-developed bump of mischief. The other donkeys, of course, would take their lead from Humphrey, but I was confident that Simon could be relied upon to provide a steadying influence. And I would be around to keep an eye on things, just in case they got out of hand. All the same my stomach was churning with apprehension when I opened the paddock gate and ushered Wailer in.

Giving a faultless impression of a duchess unexpectedly finding herself in a Hong Kong whorehouse, Wailer minced daintily past the Mafia, as I was now beginning to see them, and made his first tactical error: he turned his back on them. Humphrey, ever the opportunist, immediately sank his teeth into Wailer's beautiful backside. With an outraged yelp Wailer shot into the air then took off at a rate of knots toward the woods. Humphrey, delighted at the effect he had achieved, set off in hot pursuit closely followed by the rest of the Cosa Nostra – including, I was shocked to see, Simon. Round and round the paddock they galloped, once, twice, three times; then, just as I was about to intervene, though heaven knows what I could have done, Wailer, presumably saying the donkey equivalents of 'fainlights', gave up. He stopped dead and just stood there, a picture of submission. I looked at him in horror; I just couldn't believe that this was the elegant creature of a mere twenty minutes ago. His no-longer-haughty head hung low, his exquisitely groomed coat was daubed with mud and his silky tail looked as though it had been through the mangle. He was beginning to look like a donkey! I wanted desperately to go over and comfort him but I thought it advisable to wait until the Godfather had established his place in the hierarchy before sticking my spoke in.

Humphrey strolled over and planted himself four-square in front of Wailer. Fixing him with a no-nonsense eye he then proceeded to read him the Bill of Rights as Interpreted by Humphrey. Reduced to its basics, the gist of this was that he, Humphrey, was Top

Donkey. Nothing could be done without his say-so. As Top Donkey he was entitled not only to his own food rations but also to anybody else's he took a fancy to. He was allowed to bite other donkey's backsides but in no circumstances were other donkeys allowed to bite his. Any visitors to the paddock would be assumed to be visiting him, particularly if they came bearing goodies. Wailer would speak only when spoken to and, depending on Humphrey's mood at the time, sometimes not even then. He then went on to explain that the little dumpy non-donkey who provided food and shelter was under the impression that she was Boss and it was in all their interests to humour her in this harmless little fantasy. But she was in fact Humphrey's personal hand-maiden and any misguided attempts on the part of lesser donkeys to alter the status quo would be severely dealt with. So long as Wailer was prepared to accept these entirely reasonable precepts he would be granted Associate Membership of the Mob. With a dismissive flick of the head he turned his back on Wailer and joined the other three donkeys who were standing in a goggle-eyed group by the gate.

I went over to Wailer and made donkey-comforting noises. He raised his head and turned sad, wounded eyes on mine. With a strangled sob he buried his head in my neck and whimpered piteously. 'It's all right,' I told him. 'Take no notice of Humphrey, it's all bluff. You're one of us now and we all love you.' He looked unconvinced and I didn't blame him – I wasn't all that convinced myself. The trouble wasn't Humphrey; having made the position clear he was quite prepared to accept Wailer on the terms laid down. No, the problem lay with Wailer himself. Everything about the set-up here was strange to him. Being an only-donkey he wasn't used to donkey company, and particularly not such rough-and-ready ones as these. He didn't know how to relate to other donkeys, how to rub along with them or even how to play with them. It took a bit of getting used to. Fortunately Simon, with his affinity for the underdog, took him under his wing and provided a shoulder to cry on. But as Simon himself tended to be rather put upon by the other donkeys his patronage didn't really amount to much when it came to a confrontation. Still, at least Wailer knew that he had a friend and that was the important thing. I had long established the practice of feeding Simon separately because I knew he wouldn't get a look-in if he had to take his chances with the rest of the mob. It soon became clear that I would have to do the same with Wailer; being an incredibly dainty eater he wouldn't have stood a chance if he had to compete with the other three guzzlers. So Simon and Wailer ate together and this helped to cement the bond between them.

Once Wailer had been stripped of his elegant facade and began to look like a proper donkey he was no longer in a position to look down his nose at me. We soon established a mutually satisfying relationship which deepened over the weeks (which turned into months and eventually became two years) he was here. Because, underneath all the snootiness, he really was a very nice, rather shy little donkey. In time he joined in with the boisterous fun and games of the other donkeys and became one of the boys, but there were times when he wanted reassurance that he was an important donkey in his own right and not just one of a crowd. He needed to establish a one-to-one relationship with a non-donkey and this was where I came in. From time to time he would detach himself from the others and follow me around the paddock, tugging at my coat sleeve to get my attention. Looking anxiously into my eyes he would

52

ask, 'You do love me?' 'Of course I love you, Wailer,' I assured him, stroking his silky nose. 'You know I do.' 'Yes, but do you love me because I'm me and not just because I'm another donkey?' 'Oh Wailer,' I said. 'You're Wailer and you're special and that's why I love you. Reassured, he nuzzled my neck for a moment or two before trotting off to join the others. Sometimes I wondered what the reaction would be if I were to seek reassurance from the donkeys that they loved me for myself and not just for my food-providing capabilities. I decided not to be put it to the test.

CHAPTER 5

Living off the beaten track means that I miss out on all
sorts of things – free samples, Bingo cards, '4p-off'
coupons and all the other little treats that brighten up
the lives of town dwellers. And of course there is no
milk or paper delivery and I am still trying to find a
window cleaner intrepid enough to venture into the
hinterland. Taxi drivers are prepared to pick me up
provided I meet them at the end of the track; no way are
they going to risk damaging their tyres and exhaust
systems negotiating the pot-holed path. As the path is
littered with bits of my exhaust I can't really blame
them. Still, on the plus side I am not bothered by
Jehovah's Witnesses, salesmen and political canvas-
sers, so there is much to be thankful for. So I was a bit
nonplussed by the two men standing on the doorstep,
one tall, grey haired and rather hard-faced, the other
fat, bowler-hatted and red-faced. 'We're from the
Inland Revenue,' said the hard-faced one. 'May we
come in?' And without waiting for an answer – which he
wouldn't have got anyway because I was so shattered
I couldn't even open my mouth – he pushed past me,
followed by his companion.

Like most law-abiding, tax-paying, solid citizens

I have only to hear the words 'Inland Revenue' and I become a gibbering wreck. But I didn't see what they could possibly want with me; now that I was self-employed I had an accountant to deal with the sordid details of income tax, VAT, National Insurance Contributions and the various other tribulations visited upon those who work for themselves and which actually make the concept of 'self-employment' an absolute farce. Because the one person you are not working for is yourself – you are working for the tax man, the VAT man, the Government and the hundred and one other beaurocrats whose one aim is to make sure that the more you earn the less you keep. Not that I was such a high-flyer that I needed an accountant to control my financial empire, quite the reverse in fact. But high finance, or in my case, low finance has always had the same mystique for me as the Dead Sea Scrolls, with about the same degree of comprehensibility. I was only just beginning to come to terms with pounds, shillings and pence when They brought in decimalisation and I was back to square one again.

Where I made my big mistake was in choosing an accountant who was also a friend. On the premise that friends will be more tolerant than non-friends, my papers always ended up at the bottom of his heap. And because we enjoyed a friendly rather than a professional relationship I couldn't bring myself to complain. So things went from bad to worse until now, according to Hatchet Face, I was in Big Trouble; I had not sent in my tax return. I had not answered their letters, I had not paid the sum arbitrarily levelled in the absence of a completed return and I had not attended the Commissioner's hearing. 'Stop! Stop!' I squealed in a voice so high it seemed to be coming out of the top of my head, 'I don't know anything about this. I send everything straight on to my accountant and he deals with it.' 'Well, he hasn't done much dealing lately,' snapped Hatchet Face. 'I'll ring him,' I babbled. 'I'm sure it's all a mistake, you'll see, he'll explain everything, it's just a terrible misunderstanding.' Of course the accountant wasn't there when I rang – probably attending a non-friend's Commissioner's hearing, I reflected bitterly. His secretary said she'd get him to ring me. 'He shouldn't be more than half an hour.' 'We'll wait,' said Hatchet Face.

There followed the most uncomfortable 45 minutes of my life. 'Cup of tea?' I enquired brightly; they grunted non-committally – probably afraid of compromising themselves: 'Is the defendant seeking to impugn the integrity of these fine upstanding officials of Her Majesty's Internal Revenue Department by suggesting that they accepted inducements in the form of tea and sticky buns?' I made tea anyway, glad of something to do to pass the time. After my seventh or eighth attempt at making conversation had fizzled out, I gave up and occupied my mind wondering what prison life was like and worrying about who would look after the animals while I was serving my sentence. From time to time the appalling silence was broken by the sound of Bowler Hat slurping his tea or blowing his nose. I was intrigued by Bowler Hat; apart from an occasional ladylike 'Pardon' every time he burped, he hadn't uttered a single word. He was sitting on the edge of the sofa, resting his saucer on his enormous stomach and holding the teacup with his fat little finger daintily crooked. From time to time he looked furtively round the room, trying hard not to meet my eye. Tea finished, he extracted a large red handkerchief from his pocket and delicately wiped the cake crumbs from his rubbery lips. Meanwhile Hatchet Face was sitting bolt upright

56

in his chair, eyes fixed on a point about three inches above my head and fingers tap-tap-tapping on the chair arm. Another five minutes of this I thought and I'll go stark, raving mad.

I made one last desperate attempt at conversation and the sheer fatuousness of the words that came burbling out shows just how desperate I was. 'What a dreadful thing to happen, my goodness, just think, tax collectors calling on me for non-payment, next thing you know they'll be putting the bailiffs in, ha ha! There was a long, charged pause and then Bowler Hat said in a voice of exquisite refinement! 'Ay em the bayleaf.' I looked at him in stark horror – a bailiff, sitting in my living room, drinking my tea and eating my cakes! It was unthinkable! Respectable people don't have bailiffs calling on them in a professional capacity. Or any other capacity, for that matter. I was incensed – he hadn't even had the decency to say who he was; sitting there accepting my hospitality under false pretences. Now that he'd found his voice he went on: 'These – ahem – effects,' looking disparagingly around the room. 'Ay assume they are all paid for?' 'Of course they are,' I replied indignantly, 'I got them all at auction.' 'Yes, well, goes without saying, don't it?' he said, rather offensively to my way of thinking. 'And the – ahem – effects in the other parts of the domicile, are they of a like – ahem – quality?' 'Very like,' I snapped. 'They came from a like – ahem – source.' 'Ay see,' he said, shooting a meaningful glance at Hatchet Face. 'Well, one good thing, you won't 'ave to worry about 'aving them repossessed. There's nothing 'ere worth taking.' Thanks a bundle, that makes me feel much better. A sudden thought struck me – I could lose the cottage! If they demanded their pound of flesh and I had no other assets they could seize the cottage and I would be out on the street together with

57

five cats, five donkeys, three geese, an assortment of wild birds and beasts, countless ducks and chickens, Basil and Henrietta.

I sat there, dumbstruck with horror, willing the phone to ring. When at last it did I shot out of my chair like a bullet from a gun. The accountant must have thought I was in the final stages of dementia, squawking hysterically about tax men, bailiffs, debtors' jail, pauper's burial, all his fault . . . 'There, there,' he said soothingly, 'leave it all to me.' 'I did leave it to you,' I screamed, 'that's why I'm in all this trouble.' 'Let me talk to them, I'll soon sort it out.' I don't know what he said but it seemed to do the trick. Hatchet Face's features relaxed a smidgen and the Broker's Man's face registered a mixture of emotions which I interpreted, probably quite unjustly, as chagrin at being deprived of the pleasure of putting me out on the street and relief that he wouldn't be lumbered with my worthless – ahem – effects.

Once they'd gone my only thought was to get outside and breathe some clean fresh air. I looked all around me, at the cottage, the woods, the fields and hills, the animals and birds and I thought: 'Dear God – I could have lost it all.' It didn't bear thinking about. The donkeys, who can sense when I'm about even if they can't see me, immediately started bawling their heads off. I filled a bucket with bread and started over towards the paddock. En route I passed Gussie, who was swanning around with a wife on either side and an irrepressibly optimistic Quaggy tagging along about ten feet behind. The goose situation was working out splendidly; Suzie and Esme had settled in immediately and Gussie was his old obnoxious self again, throwing his weight about and chasing me around the pond. The only problem, so far as Gussie was concerned, was

Esme. He had made it clear, right from the start, that any attempts on the part of his paramours to fraternise with the enemy (namely me) would be severely dealt with. Suzie accepted this meekly enough but Esme considered that, after a lifetime of servitude, she had earned the right to do her own thing and wasn't about to be dictated to by some whippersnapper a fraction of her age. She never openly defied him, she just ignored him, which Gussie found absolutely infuriating.

I had become inordinately fond of this spirited old lady; what she lacked in youth and looks she more than made up for in character. As soon as she saw me she came trotting over and, rubbing her knobbly head against my legs, said, 'Honk,' meaning 'Bread, please.' I gave her a slice which she munched happily; meanwhile Gussie was jumping up and down in a frenzy screaming, 'Come back here AT ONCE.' Esme, giving no sign that she had ever heard him, finished her bread and said 'Honk, honk,' which I took to mean 'another slice please. Not for eating, just for carrying around.' She has a deep-rooted 'never-know-where-your-next-meal's-coming-from' complex and never feels really secure unless she had a slice of break in her mouth 'just in case.' And she resolutely refuses to go to bed at night without her food reserve, presumably as insurance against a sudden attack on night starvation. Gussie, fuming with frustration, makes a move towards us, then stops; he has a problem. If he doesn't put his foot down firmly and show Esme who is Boss the situation could get completely out of hand. He would lose face, the other birds would despise him and his position as overlord would be severely threatened. But if he engages in a confrontation now Suzie will be left alone and vulnerable to Quaggy's amorous advances. The same thought has obviously occurred to Quaggy who is watching Gussie hopefully, waiting to grab his opportunity. Gussie wavers for a moment or two while he considers the position. Then, mind made up, he comes charging over determined to settle this nonsense once and for all. He can deal with Quaggy later – first things first. Eyes blazing, he gives Esme a spine-chilling account of the likely fate awaiting a senile goose foolhardy enough to defy her lord and master. Esme doesn't even look up; she has no intention of going anywhere until she has her emergency rations. I hurriedly give her another piece of bread, before Gussie decides that it's all my fault and turns his attentions to me. He is already eyeing me with a gleam that bodes no good and I feel an enormous surge of admiration for Esme's courage. To my relief she turns and starts walking unhurriedly towards the pond followed by a vociferously expostulating Gussie. I thank God I'm not on the receiving end of his diatribe, but Esme just lets it all roll over her. As long as she's got her slice-of-bread comforter in her mouth nothing can touch her.

The donkeys, fast losing patience, add their unlovely voices to Gussie's querulous serenade and the ducks and chickens, outraged at my partisanship, stick in their two penn'orth. I throw them some bread and wonder, not for the first time, how the myth of the quiet peaceful countryside ever gained currency. I also wonder, as I do every day, just where the day has gone. The hours slip by and before I know it it's evening and I've achieved nothing. Tomorrow will be different, I vow. Tomorrow I will not be deflected. Tomorrow I will Get Things Done. I don't know who I think I'm kidding, as I know that tomorrow will be exactly the same as today and yesterday and all the other yesterdays, but at least it shows willing.

I eventually reach the donkeys, who are giving a

moving impression of being in the terminal stages of starvation and neglect. They inspect the bucket of bread morosely – you managed to save us some, then? I rub four noses and one shaggy backside (Simon has a backside fixation) and explain that there was a Crisis. 'When isn't there?' they reply. There's no answer to that, and to prove it Castor comes running over clucking miserably. No need to ask her what's wrong – the fact that she's on her own says it all. She and Pollux, the other Polish bantam, are inseparable; where one goes, there goes the other. I pick her up and she climbs onto my shoulder; beak about half an inch from my ear, she tells me all her troubles. The gist of her message is that Pollux has gone. 'Don't worry,' I say, with a confidence I am far from feeling. 'We'll find her.' Of course, she could be nesting but in that case Castor would be with her. Last year they had made a communal nest and sat together, bringing up the resultant babies as one family. Was it possible that, while I was reluctantly entertaining Hatchet Face and the Broker's Man, a fox had seized his opportunity and made off with Pollux?

With Castor still on my shoulder I started on a tour of the garden, the paddock, the ditches, the shed, the barn and the donkey shelter. When I had nowhere else to look I started again at the beginning, just in case I'd missed her the first time around. 'Where are you, Pollux,' I bawled. 'Pollux, Pollux, Pollux.' 'Cluck Cluck Cluck,' echoed Castor mournfully. I was on my second circuit of the paddock when I noticed a man leaning on the gate and watching me with some interest. 'Dear God,' I pleaded, 'not more callers, I couldn't stand it.' He continued to watch me as I made my way over to the gate and shot him an enquiring look. He looked straight back. 'Was that you shouting rude

61

words?' he asked. I was stunned. 'What are you talking about? I was looking for a missing chicken.' All at once it struck me and I added defensively 'Her name is Pollux.' He considered this for a moment or two and then, with a glance at Castor remarked, 'Oh aye. And I suppose this one's called cobblers?' I shot him a sharp look and noticed a twitch at the corner of his mouth, then we both gave a yell of delight and fell about laughing. It was just what I needed to exorcise the memory of Hatchet Face and Broker's Man.

When we'd got our breath back he said 'Come on, I'll help you look for her. My name's Alf Turner', and in fact it was he who eventually found Pollux cowering under the shed, shivering with fright and nursing a broke wing. 'Poor little bugger,' he crooned, cradling her in a hand the size of a bunch of bananas. 'You've got your troubles and that's a fact. Not surprising, with a name like that! Pollux I ask you!' And he was off again. I didn't dare catch his eye or he'd have got me going too. Pulling himself together he set to work expertly splinting Pollux's wing with a couple of sticks and a bandage from my medicine chest. 'There you go,' he said, 'You'll soon be right as ninepence.' Castor, who has been watching anxiously, gave a cluck of delight and trotted after us into the kitchen. She fussed and fretted while I installed Pollux in a box to recuperate then, with a quizzical glance at me, hopped in with her. 'Oh, all right,' I said. 'Just this once.'

Bustling around making tea for my Good Samaritan I reflected on the mad whirl of social activity I had suddenly been plunged into; three callers in one day! How long can I hold up under the pressure? I asked myself. Alf told me that he lived in the next village and was In Pigs. What a nice class of friends I'm making, I mused; sewage workers, pig breeders. Just as Mr

Sludge was devoted to his sewage so Alf was in love with his pigs. For the next half hour my head whirled under a bombardment of brucellosis, swine fever, erysipelas, gilts, farrowing, swill, weaners. 'A weaner!' he suddenly shouted. 'That's what you want, a little weaner.' I looked at him in horror – I didn't want anything of the sort. In fact, if there was one single thing I didn't want, that was it. 'You don't understand,' he insisted. 'A little weaner will clear all the roots and weeds and undergrowth in that jungle out there, even better than a plough. Then, when the little fellow's done the job you give it back to me.' Oh no, I thought, you don't catch me like that. I knew just what would happen – I would become attached to my piggy-gardener and wouldn't be able to part with him when the time came. Before I knew it I would be playing foster-mum to a two-ton hog. And it wouldn't end there; soon I would start worrying about my charge's emotional well-being and agonising over the cruelty of keeping him on his own, so I would have to get him a mate. In no time at all I would be knee-deep in tiny pink porkers, none of whom I could bear to see transmuted into pork chops, rashers of bacon and prime ham. Oh dear me, no!

'At least come and see them,' pleaded Alf. 'You'll soon change your mind.' 'Yes, that's what I'm afraid of,' I told him. 'And that's why I'm absolutely determined not to come within a mile of them.' Piglets in the abstract I could resist; a piglet in the flesh was a different kettle of swill entirely. One look and I'd be lost. Seeing that my mind was made up, Alf gave in. 'But I still think you're making a big mistake,' he said sorrowfully. 'Not half as big a mistake as I'd be making if I let you talk me into it,' I thought. After he'd gone I found myself musing somewhat wistfully about the piglet that wasn't to be. I took myself in hand; I had done the right thing, for once, and in fact I was rather pleased with myself for having been so firm and resolute. Could it be that I was learning, at last?

CHAPTER 6

'Come on puddies,' I said, brushing the cats off my lap, 'time to get Basil's supper.' Basil, perched on the curtain rail, turned his button eyes on me and nodded approvingly. I went out to the kitchen to get his food and when I came back I was amazed to see that he was back on his perch, head nodding in gleeful anticipation. He was very much a creature of habit, refusing to eat anywhere except on his perch. But how had he got up there? He usually waited for me to give him a lift-up. Over the next few days I noticed that he was becoming much more venturesome in his jaunts round the room; instead of breaking up his journey into four legs he was now doing it in two, and he had no difficulty in flying up to his perch. There was no doubt about it, his wing was getting stronger. Was it possible that the vet had been over-cautious in his prognosis and that Basil would be fit enough to go eventually? 'Oh Basil,' I enthused, 'Wouldn't it be marvellous if you could go back to the wild?' He looked up for a moment, bits of disgusting fur clinging to his beak like a moustache, then re-addressed himself to his food. Suddenly my heart plummeted; even if his wing healed completely how could I possibly give such a soft, sloppy, jelly-baby of a bird his freedom? Bird of prey? He was nothing but an overgrown budgie in kestrel's clothing. He wouldn't last five minutes in the wild. It was my fault, I should never have let him become so tame. True, I wasn't to know that he would confound medical science, but the fact that I had acted in good faith would avail him little when he found himself looking down the business end of a gun barrel. At the same time, I couldn't keep a perfectly fit bird permanently captive. There was only one thing for it – he would have to be dehumanised.

I set to work building a large outside enclosure, sited well away from the cottage so that his contact with people would be minimal. My hope was that while his wing was getting stronger his ties with people would become weaker so that by the time he was ready to go his old aggressive instincts would have re-established themselves. A forlorn hope, I knew, but worth a try. When his new home was ready I put some food in it and went into the cottage to get Basil. He hopped onto my shoulder and I thought, 'This is the last time we'll do this.' But I couldn't bring myself to turf him into the enclosure and just shut the door on him: 'Just one last walk round the garden, Basil,' I told him, then brought myself up short. That must be the last time I used his name; he wasn't Basil, he was an injured wild bird who would soon be well enough to be released. This was going to be a lot harder than I'd thought. After a final, farewell tour of the garden and paddock I took him into the enclosure, settled him on a perch and walked out without a word. From then on, except for feeding him and changing his water, I left him strictly alone. Twice a day I poked his food through the wire netting and walked quickly away so that I wouldn't be tempted to look at him or talk to him. He came to terms with the situation far more quickly than I did; after a few days moping he perked up and started taking an interest in the world outside his wire prison. The big break-through came when he stopped swooping across when he saw me coming with his food; he would watch warily as I shoved it through the netting, then wait till I'd gone before taking it. Over the new few weeks I was over-joyed to see him flying around his enclosure, his wing getting stronger with every day that passed. You'll soon be ready to go, I thought.

By now it was high summer and the hot sunny days were heavy with the smell of honeysuckle and new mown hay, tinged with the occasional whiff of pig manure from a neighbouring farm. Birds were busily nesting, butterflies and bees were darting thither and yon and once again I was up to eyeballs in baby chicks. As Clara, the retarded bantam, still persisted in laying her eggs on the barn roof her chances of raising a family were pretty remote. Previously I had set her on a clutch of ducks eggs, the ducks showing no inclination to sit on their eggs themselves, and she had reared a pair of ducklings. But remembering the traumas she had suffered every time they went on the pond, I decided not to repeat the experiment. Then Alec gave me a clutch of pheasant eggs and I thought they'd be just the job for Clara; after all, pheasant breeders use bantams to incubate their eggs. As before, I made a nest in the barn and installed Clara on it; when the eggs hatched I don't know which of us was the more thrilled. It didn't last long, alas. What I hadn't realised was that pheasant chicks become independent of their mums within a matter of days and despite Clara's despairing calls and entreaties they insisted on going their own way. It broke my heart to see her trotting after them, imploring them to come back so that she could protect them from

67

the perils awaiting hapless chicks who face the world alone. They took not a scrap of notice.

I was bitterly ashamed at the unhappiness I had caused her, albeit unwittingly, and as soon as she went broody again I put her on a clutch of bantam eggs. She hatched all twelve of them, and there never was a prouder mother. The only trouble was that the call of the barn roof was still strong within her and she couldn't understand why the babies, still only a few days old, didn't follow her. The chicks for their part couldn't understand why their Mother Hen thought she was a stork. For the first week I had to stand guard over the little ones while mum was on the barn roof calling them. Eventually Clara got the message and resigned herself to the fact that she would have to be grounded while the babies were still tiny. But the minute they were big enough she was back on the roof, surrounded by her twelve offspring and clucking happily. Suzie, too, had got the baby bug; she had laid three eggs and was sitting on them, fiercely guarded by the proud father-to-be. Shortly after, to my amazement, and I suspect to hers too, Esme followed suit and produced one oddly shaped egg. She regarded the fruit of her loins with some misgiving then, after pondering for a moment or two, came to a decision. Gently nudging it with her beak, she rolled the egg over to where Suzie was sitting and carefully tucked it under her. I couldn't blame her – who in their right mind would want all the hassle of bringing up a child in their dotage?

With the summer, as with every other season, came a problem. But this was one I certainly hadn't anticipated. After living in the caravan for almost two years and in a small, easily maintained flat for eight years before that, I was totally unprepared for the amount of

68

housework involved in keeping a house going. At best my housekeeping can only be described as hit and miss; you do it today and it needs doing all over again tomorrow – what's the point? I have the greatest admiration for people like my sister; you can call on her unannounced at any time of the day or night and her house will be immaculate – not a speck of dust or a misplaced cushion anywhere. Me, I need two months notice if I'm having guests. Of course she hasn't got five cats wiping their muddy paws on the carpets and wild birds doing unmentionable things all over the furniture, I tell myself defensively, but I know that isn't the answer – she's just got it all together and I haven't. During that long hot summer I found myself getting more and more resentful at the time I seemed to be spending just keeping on top of the housework – time which I would much rather have spent outside. And then I had what I can only describe as a stroke of sheer inspiration. Why waste precious daylight hours on boring household chores when they can be done just as well at night? In fact, they could probably be done better at night, as I wouldn't be wasting time looking longingly out of the window wishing I could be out there. One night a week, I decided, I wouldn't go to bed; I would stay up and get as many of the household jobs as possible out of the way. With the odd bad-weather day we can usually depend on even in the best of summers I should be able to keep the housework from getting out of hand. Monday, I decided, would be my bedless night. Barmy? In my saner moments I thought so too, but in fact it turned out to be the most inspired decision I have ever made, opening up a whole new world to me.

On moonlit nights I would watch the owls hunting in the woods, and the foxes going about their business; as

69

dawn broke Muntjac deer could be seen at the edge of the woods, and shortly after pheasants appeared from nowhere, searching for food in the paddock. And two pairs of partridges with their little ones in tow. These night watches provided some of the most intensely satisfying moments of my life. The housework? Well, there were always the hours before dawn and the moonless nights! The only snag was that the donkeys, with their uncanny instinct for anything a bit out of the ordinary going on, always sussed me out on these night patrols. Naturally assuming that if I was out and about at this extraordinary hour it could be for only one purpose, i.e. to bring them sustenance, they immediately set up an unholy row, braying excitedly to let me know that I was expected. This of course set off the ducks and geese and chickens, with the result that any wildlife in the immediate vicinity promptly took off in search of quieter environs. I eventually got around this problem by keeping a supply of donkey food on hand so that I could shovel it into them before they had a chance to give voice. It didn't always work, but at least it gave me chances

Charlie and Pudding were enchanted at the idea of walkies in the middle of the night and always came with me; so did Flossie at first, but then I noticed that she was starting to hang back. If I stopped and waited for her to catch up, she stopped too. After a while she gave up coming altogether. She was also a bit diffident about coming into the house, looking all around the kitchen through the cat-flap before venturing in. I soon found out why. Charlie, for some reason known only to himself, had suddenly taken agin her and was making her life a misery. He wouldn't allow her in the cottage if he was there; if he caught sight of her in the garden he was after her like a shot and soon the air was thick with

feline oaths and imprecations. I still think that if Flossie
had stood her ground and refused to be intimidated the
situation would have resolved itself but this just wasn't
her way. Immediately she caught sight of Charlie she
turned tail and fled and of course Charlie fled after her. I
was appalled; one of the basic precepts of the set-up
here is that everybody – donkeys, geese, ducks, cats,
whatever – has to get on with everybody else otherwise
life would be untenable. I recalled, with a shudder, the
fraught months when Percy, the guinea fowl, was with
us. His pathological hatred of every other living
creature, furred, feathered and human, had brought us
all to the brink of complete nervous collapse. I couldn't
go through all that again. True, Charlie didn't hate
everybody, only Flossie, but this could be just the
beginning. Already the other cats, taking their cue from

71

Charlie, were starting to gang up on her and I was having to feed her in the barn because they wouldn't allow her in the house. Soon she started disappearing, at first just for a day or two, then for a week or more. Distraught, I spent days searching for her, knowing that my efforts were futile; why would she want to come home when she knew she would simply be chased off again.

After Flossie had been missing for almost two weeks I had a phone call for Melina, Graham Christie's wife. She had heard that I had lost a cat, was it by any chance a fat tabby? If so it had taken up residence with her. I chased over and there was Flossie happily installed in the most comfortable armchair and surrounded by Melina's besotted children. Melina told me that she had found Flossie in their barn and assumed she was a stray, 'though I'll admit she did look a bit fat for a stray.' Anyway, they had all fallen in love with her and she was now one of the family. I looked at Flossie, relaxed and content and enjoying the unaccustomed homage being paid to her, then at the wistful faces of the children. This, surely, was the answer? I explained the position to Melina and said that if she would consider keeping Flossie she would be doing her, and me, an enormous service. I didn't have to wait for an answer – the relief and joy on their faces said it all.

On the journey home I made a conscious effort to keep those enraptured faces in my mind, to counteract the dreadful sense of loss and guilt I felt. I recalled my sentiments when I had seen the small-ad offering Phil and Sophie 'free to a good home.' What sort of person gives away their donkeys I had wondered. Well, what sort of person gives away their cat? But this is different, I told myself. Flossie has gone to a loving home, with people you know and where she'll be happy and cared for. She chose this home herself, obviously preferring it to the misery of her old home. Be happy for her. I was happy for her – I was just miserable for myself. During the first year Flossie came back for fleeting visits three or four times; she never stayed long – after about an hour, during which time she visited all her old haunts and hunting grounds, she took off happily across the fields to her new home. What I found most odd about the whole business was that the Christies have hordes of cats, some of them quite beautiful, but they are strictly farm cats. Only Flossie is allowed inside the house to be pampered and spoilt rotten.

CHAPTER 7

I woke up with a sense of impending doom and scrabbled around frantically in my mind trying to remember what it was about today that had got my subconscious into such a dither. Then it struck me and my heart sank. It was hoof-trimming day. Now that I was a donkey-owner on a relatively large scale I no longer had to take them down to Julia's to have their hooves trimmed; the blacksmith came to me – an arrangement which I suspect caused Julia very little grief. I absolutely dread hoof-trimming day; all the donkeys have to be caught and tied to the fence, ready and waiting when Mr Regan, the blacksmith, arrives. The first one isn't too bad because I can usually catch it unawares and have the head collar on and tied to the fence before the captive realises what's going on. But the remaining four, having had a preview of coming events, don't hang around awaiting their turn – they're off at the first sight of the halter. Phil, Sophie and Wailer are fairly easy to catch – a carrot or an apple usually does the trick. Humphrey, on principle, never does anything the easy way. He is quite prepared to be caught, tied and pedicured but only on his terms. His terms involved a half-hour chase around the paddock, dragging me along the ground for about fifteen yards, knocking me over at least twice and, given half a chance, putting the boot in. Honour satisfied, he happily thrusts his head into the collar and stands quietly by while I tie him up. He is conserving his energy for Part Two of this Everyday Story of Bloody-Minded Donkeys. I catch the gleam in his eye and my heart bleeds for Tim Regan – or used to. Until I realised that Tim, for all his short stature and very slight frame, wasn't one to be put upon by donkeys with exaggerated ideas of their place in society. He didn't stand for any nonsense from his infinitely classier, more highly bred clients so he certainly wasn't going to take it from some misbegotten moke.

I remember the first time he called to do the donkeys' feet; Humphrey took one look at him and decided that here was someone he could have a bit of fun with. A little bloke like that? He could take him with one hoof tied behind his back! As soon as Tim approached Humphrey jerked his head back, catching him an almighty wallop on the nose and pulling the rope free from the fence – knot-tying has never been one of my strong points. Once free, he took off at a gallop, with Tim clinging on to the rope for dear life. I watched, gaping and goggle-eyed as Humphrey hauled Tim around the paddock, once, twice, three times. Most of the time Tim's feet weren't even touching the ground, but he hung on grimly. The Wild West was never like this! After what seemed like several hours to me, and heaven only knows what it must have seemed like to Tim, Humphrey stopped abruptly and, giving every impression of capitulation, allowed himself to be tied up. Immediately Tim let go of his head and he lashed out wildly with his back legs, giving Tim a vicious kick in the shins. Tim promptly kicked him back. I was

aghast – Humphrey would surely kill him or, at best, kick him playfully around the paddock. For a moment Humphrey was so stunned that he just stood there, not moving a muscle. He's dead, I thought. He's had a heart-attack, it's the shock. The message hasn't reached his legs yet – when it does, he'll fall down. Then Humphrey very slowly turned his head and looked Tim straight in the eye. I held my breath as Tim stared straight back. They held the gaze for a moment or two, then Humphrey lowered his eyes. He was admitting defeat! I never thought I'd live to see the day. Since then Tim has had no trouble with Humphrey – or at least, not much. Humphrey still tries it on from time to time, more to keep his hand in than anything else, but one word from Tim and he soon gets the message.

This morning was no different from any other hoof-trimming morning. I always made catching them the first job of the day, while I was still relatively bright-eyed and bushy-tailed. I knew it would take every scrap of energy I had, so there was no point in dissipating this increasingly diminishing commodity on other, less pressing matters such as feeding the birds and cats, not to mention myself. Of course, the other beasts didn't see it quite this way, their priorities being rather different from mine. Tough luck, I told them – a little self-denial never hurt anyone. After an hour I had four donkeys lined up in a neat row and tethered to the fence. I took a deep breath – time now for the Big One. Because, unbelievably, soft, gentle easy-going Simon was always the hardest to catch and the last to be tethered – indeed, more often than not he was still uncaught and untethered when Tim Regan arrived and Tim was not only obliged to put on his Ride-'em-Cowboy act, he frequently had to call in reinforcements.

I could understand and fully sympathise with Simon's behaviour. The ill-treatment he had suffered in his early days had left mental scars that would never fully heal. The sight of a rope or a stick brought it all back to him, opening up old wounds and sending him into a frenzy. My heart ached for him and I wondered, as I wondered every time we went through this performance, how anyone could possibly beat a donkey, and particularly such a sweet-natured donkey as Simon. I was saddened to think that even after all this time together and despite the trust we had built up, the sight of a rope in my hand could strike such terror in him. It was especially painful to know that I was the cause of his present fear. Because of this, I usually didn't make too much of an effort to catch him; my chances of success were minimal anyway, and I couldn't bear to see the hurt and fear in his eyes and know that I was responsible for them. Much better to leave it to a comparative stranger and not risk damaging the fragile bond that had taken so long to build up between us.

When Tim arrived he glanced at the four tethered donkeys and, with a raised eyebrow, enquired 'Simon?' 'Simon,' I confirmed. He sighed deeply and turning to his assistant said, 'Come on, Donny – rodeo time.' Deploying Donny and me in strategic spots as long stops he set off in pursuit of Simon. The plan was to get him into the donkey shelter; Tim would drive him in and Donny and I would cut off his retreat. But of course, having been through this many times before, Simon knew the plan as well as we did and nothing would induce him to go anywhere near the shelter. After the second circuit of the paddock I was fit to drop; and chain-smoking years were catching up on me and I was puffing like grampus. Simon, on the other hand, looked as fresh as a daisy and was obviously prepared to carry on all day if needs be. I don't know what would have happened if Humphrey hadn't suddenly stepped backwards, pulling his rope taut across Simon's path. Simon breasted the rope and stopped short, and Tim and I threw up our hands and yelled, 'The winner!' We fell on Simon and got the head collar on before he had a chance to recover his equilibrium. Tom tied him up and, at long last, got down to the real purpose of his visit – trimming their hooves. I left him to it and went inside to put the kettle on. Over a cup of tea I made my customary apologies. I was always terribly embarrassed about the whole business and my one fear was that Tim would eventually decide that he hadn't served a long, exhaustive apprenticeship learning his craft only to find himself rounding up runaway donkeys, and refuse to come again. Not at all, said Tim. He thoroughly enjoyed his sessions with the donkeys, indeed looked forward to them. They were a challenge. Well, that was one way of looking at it.

This was the time of year when racing pigeons started arriving by the barrow load. They were almost all youngsters on their first flight and suffering from exhaustion. Some of them were very small and I couldn't help wondering whether they were really up to it yet. I always rang the relevant society, giving them details of the bird's serial number but more often than not the owner didn't bother to contact me and I would keep the bird until it was strong enough to leave. I don't know how true it is, but someone once told me that racing pigeons that failed to return on time were usually destroyed by their owners, who saw no point in feeding and caring for birds that would never make the grade. Presumably these same owners also saw no point in coming to collect birds that were destined for the chop, so they simply washed their hands of them. Some of these pigeons were brought to me by people who had come across them lying exhausted by the side of the road; others came under their own steam, breaking their journey to spend a few days recuperating on the barn roof, and quite a few I picked up myself while I was out and about. Undoubtedly the luckiest of these was the one I found tottering about drunkenly on the hard shoulder of the M1 – one false move and he would have met a nasty end under the wheels of a juggernaut. Praying fervently that I wouldn't be spotted by a police patrol, I pulled in and picked him up. Incredibly, a few miles further on I spotted a hedgehog meandering along on the hard shoulder, again perilously close to the traffic on the inside lane. It is so rare these days to see a hedgehog actually on the move and not squashed flat by a heedless motorist that I couldn't bear to leave it to its inevitable fate. I scooped him up, popped him in a box and took him home with me. It occurred to me that I might be depriving a hedgehog family of its bread-winner, but on reflection decided that an absentee head of household was preferable to a dead one. Brian, as I dubbed him, settled in splendidly in the garden, eventually finding himself a wife and producing a brood of delightful little loo brushes.

Meanwhile Gussie was exulting in the unaccustomed role of father. Only two of Suzie's eggs had hatched and while I was delighted for the proud parents, I was a bit dismayed to see that they were virtual clones of Gussie, right down to his uncertain temper and grouchy temperament. Although they were no bigger than a grapefruit, they already had Gussie's snapping beak and neck-along-the-ground routine down to a fine art. Esme had assumed the role of nanny and universal

79

aunt, sharing with Suzie the joys and woes of rearing a family.

The influx of injured and exhausted birds was placing an enormous strain on my limited facilities – no sooner did I build a new enclosure than along came a casualty to occupy it. I decided that the time had come to stop shilly-shallying and give Basil the freedom he was now ready for; no more excuses (it's too cold, it's too warm, he looks a little pale today, the weather forecast said rain, etc. etc . . .). Do it NOW! I fed him early in the morning and took him over to the field where Alec had found him. He hopped on to the gate-post and looked all around him, presumably trying to get his bearings. When I moved away he looked round but made no attempt to follow me – the dehumanising programme had obviously been effective. What was needed now, I told myself wryly, was a dekestrelising programme – I knew I was going to miss him dreadfully. I hid behind the hedge and watched as he flapped his wings and then, to my delight, he suddenly took off, flying and wheeling over the field. He made two circuits of the field then landed on the gate-post; a few minutes rest and he was off again. I went inside and, from the kitchen window, watched him swooping and soaring across the field, clearly exulting in his freedom. At his usual feeding time I took out some meat for him. He was sitting on the gatepost waiting for me and obviously hungry as he gobbled the meat greedily. I was a bit sad that he hadn't managed to catch his own supper but it was early days yet.

For the next seven to eight days Basil waited for me on the gate-post, night and morning. Sometimes he was hungry, other times not, so he was at least catching some food. Then he started missing a visit, then two or three until at last he stopped coming altogether. But I

80

still saw him from time to time, circling the field and enjoying life to the full. When at last he brought a female companion with him I knew that he had become fully rehabilitated and I rejoiced for him.

I put up the 'accommodation vacant' sign on Basil's enclosure and awaited developments. These weren't long in coming, although they were a bit unexpected. Jim Barrie, my RSPCA inspector friend, rang to say that he was coming up from Wales and would be bringing a convalescent buzzard for me to care for. Would that be OK? A buzzard I didn't know much about buzzards but what little I did know, or thought I knew, I didn't much like. They were cruel, aggressive birds with huge beaks and ugly features. On reflection, I think I might have been confusing them with vultures, because Buzby was nothing like my mental image of buzzards. For one thing, he was one of the most handsome birds I have seen – beautifully marked and with a touch of grandeur about his superbly shaped head. But the biggest surprise was to discover that, far from being aggressive, he was almost painfully shy, going to ridiculous lengths to make himself invisible if a stranger came anywhere near his enclosure; 'You're just an old softie,' I told him. He peered shyly back at me: 'I know, but let's just keep it between ourselves.' Jim told me that Buzby had been poisoned and when he first came into his care his neck was rigid and his head twisted behind his back. He was over the worst but the shock had resulted in the loss of his tail feathers so he couldn't fly. It was just a question of keeping him until they grew back again, then he could go back to Wales for release. This isn't buzzard country and his chances of survival if he were released here would be virtually nil.

Two weeks later Buzby was joined by Leighton Buzzard. Incredible, I thought. You go through the greater part of your life without ever meeting a buzzard and then suddenly they start arriving in droves. I put him in with Buzby and was delighted to see they took to each other immediately. Thank goodness birds aren't like people, I thought, taking instant dislikes to one another, judging others by their clothes or their education or their accents. Much more sensible this way, accepting anybody so long as they are the same species. Leighton's wing was very badly damaged and it seemed likely that he would be a permanent resident. I was a bit worried about how he would react when his cell-mate left, but decided to worry about that when the time came.

I was outside feeding the buzzards one autumn day when I noticed what looked like a badly-packed parachute ambling up the path. As it drew nearer I saw that it was actually a woman wearing an extraordinary conglomeration of oddly-matched clothes – a long ethnic skirt with a shorter woolly one over it, smock, cardy and poncho over her shoulders, and tout ensemble topped off with a shaggy straw hat. Well, to each his own, I thought. Instead of continuing along the path towards the woods, to my surprise she made a beeline for me. Do I know her, I wondered? It seemed unlikely; true, my appalling memory for faces is matched only by my equally appalling memory for names, but even so I was quite sure I couldn't forget anyone quite as – well – distinctive as this. She stopped abruptly in front of the buzzards' enclosure, to their considerable alarm. I sympathised with them – to birds as nervous as these she must have represented the last word in horror. Without so much as a how-d'you-do she barked, 'Disgusting! Wild birds in cages is a sin against nature. We did not throw off our manacles in order to stand by and watch our weaker sisters forced into captivity.' Oh Lord, I thought, not one of those. I find I have very little in common with women like this – the kind somebody once described as 'No bra and a lot of unsupported opinions to match.' 'Not sisters, brothers, actually,' I told her. 'They're fellas', 'Don't quibble,' snapped Droopy-Boobs. 'The fight goes on. We shall not rest until the chains have gone throughout the world. Throw open the doors and let these brave spirits fly free!' With an effort I controlled my immediate impulse, which was to throw open the doors and sling her in with these brave spirits; the only reason I didn't was because Buzby and Leighton had done nothing to deserve such a fate. I counted to ten and then said, very slowly and very carefully, 'These birds are here because they are sick or injured. If you release

them they will die, either from their injuries or because they are unable to fend for themselves or at the hands of some lunatic with a gun. When they are fit they will be released.' To me this sounded like a pretty reasonable argument and I fully expected her to subside immediately and beg my forgiveness. What I hadn't taken into account was that fanatics are not reasonable people – if they were, they wouldn't be fanatics. To my amazement she cried, 'Better death than a lifetime of servitude!' 'Oh come on now,' I protested, 'If you want to choose death over captivity for yourself, fair enough. But what gives you the right to make life or death decisions for other, more helpless creatures?' Her face turned purple and I really thought she was going to do herself a mischief. 'It is because they are helpless and cannot speak for themselves that they need a Voice,' she thundered. 'I am that Voice!'

Really, I asked myself, why am I wasting time arguing with her – I had a very real fear that she would come back late one night and release all my 'brave' spirits', thereby sentencing them to certain death, and possibly a long and painful one at that. I can identify strongly with the ideals of animal liberationists – to see the end of battery hens, calves intensively bred for veal, unnatural methods of pig littering, forced feeding of geese for pâté de fois gras and the many other abuses we so-called higher creatures subject animals to in the cause of improved food production. What I can't come to terms with is the methods they use to gain their ends. Surely if you're hoping to persuade people to come around to your point of view, the worst thing you can do is to antagonise them. I'm not suggesting that sweet reason would necessarily work, after all farmers and breeders can hardly be expected to embrace whole-heartedly a cause that will cost them money, but at least it wouldn't be counterproductive, which their present methods certainly are. The sad thing is that these extremists are antagonising people who can help their cause, who sympathise with their aims but not with their methods, because their extreme actions are rarely in the best interests of the animals themselves. It is hardly an act of kindness to free animals who have never known freedom and so are ill-equipped to deal with it; to leave them to find their own food and shelter in a world full of predators – both animal and human. Just as farmers have to be persuaded rather than bullied into using more humane methods, so the animals themselves need to be brought up to freedom and not have it thrust upon them.

This was brought home to me very forcefully when I saw a notice outside a chicken farm offering clapped-out battery hens for sale. After about two years these hens are past their productive best and are replaced by younger ones. What a wonderful opportunity, I thought naively – to take these birds out of slavery and let them spend their remaining years in a free and natural environment. I bought six and, in a state of high excitement, took them home. I couldn't wait to see their joy when I released them and they realised they were free to roam wherever they chose, to dig for worms and roll in the dust, to hide their eggs – even to sit on them if they wanted to. But not immediately – first they must become acclimatised. I put them into a chicken house with a long run and waited to see how they would react to the comparative freedom. They reacted all right, but not the way I expected. They were absolutely terrified by all the space around them. They crawled into the farthest corner of the chicken house and sat there all day, huddled together and shivering with fright. If I put food under their noses they would eat it; if I scattered it in the run it just stayed there, untouched.

On the fourth day I left the food just outside the door of the chicken house and waited to see what happened. After about half an hour one wary beak emerged, took a tentative peck at the food and shot back in again. A few minutes later it appeared again and took another peck before disappearing inside. After another few moments two beaks emerged and then a third. Soon there were six beaks tucking in. The following day I put the food a little further away and was delighted to see that all six chickens were venturing out to get it. But there was something most unchickenlike about their behaviour; they didn't jostle each other or scrabble about looking for the choicest titbits – they just stood there in a solid phalanx eating whatever was under their noses. I soon discovered why they stood so close together – their legs were so weak they couldn't stand up without some sort of support. Looking at them, thin, scraggy and barely feathered, wobbling about helplessly on legs that had  forgotten how to walk – if they had ever known – I wondered whether I was really doing them a kindness by liberating them. It was all very well for me to talk airily and sanctimoniously about 'freedom', but it was just a word; it had no meaning for these pathetic chickens. I'll give them three weeks, I decided, and if they show no signs of improvement I'll have them painlessly put down.

Over the next week or two I watched them closely and was overjoyed to see that they were putting on weight and their feathers were growing back. Soon they started coming out immediately they heard the rattle of the food bucket; they were still a big shaky on their legs but they could stand unaided. They began to spend longer and longer periods in the enclosure until eventually they were outside all day, only going into the chicken house to sleep. And they began to roost. At first they kept falling off the perch but as their feet grew stronger and their confidence returned, they soon got the hang of it.

About six weeks after they came I looked at them and my heart swelled; they were fat, perky, glossy-feathered and, to my way of thinking anyway, absolutely beautiful. Time to integrate them. I opened the enclosure door and left it to them to decide whether or not they wanted to come out. The first day they decided they didn't. The second day they thought they might just stick their noses outside, just to get the feel of things. It wasn't until the third day that they took the plunge and actually ventured into the world outside. I watched from a window as they took the first tentative steps; a pause for reflection and a cautious look-round, followed by a hastily convened conference. Agreement reached, they picked their way carefully towards an apparently predetermined spot and settled down comfortably to enjoy the scenery. Two minutes later their peaceful sojourn was disrupted by what I took to be a whirling dervish but which, on closer inspection, turned out to be Josh, the bantam cockerel. Overjoyed at these additions to his harem, and without so much as a by-your-leave, he set to work making them welcome in his own inimitable way. Sex not having previously reared its ugly head, the newcomers were taken completely by surprise as he enthusiastically worked his way through them, one by one. Their faces took on a faraway, contemplative look – 'I don't know what all that was about but I think I could learn to like it.' Following these initiation rites they became fully paid-up members of the chicken community, eating and sleeping and coexisting with the other birds. And

they started laying – big, beautiful orange-yolked eggs
fit for the gods. They enjoyed many happy productive
years of freedom and I was delighted that it had worked
out so well. But I learned the hard way that good
intentions alone are not enough, and that unaccustomed freedom can be just as frightening to an animal as
unaccustomed imprisonment.

CHAPTER 8

'Blast him,' I muttered, frantically clearing out cupboards, polishing cutlery, cleaning windows and trying to catch up on all the other household chores that somehow keep sliding to the bottom of the heap. 'Why can't he come on Visiting Days like everybody else?' Three times a year, Christmas, autumn and spring (but never summer!), I set aside a few days for formal entertaining. By this I mean entertaining people for whom a spring-cleaning session is necessary. Having got the cottage into pristine condition I get all my entertaining over in one fell swoop and then don't have to worry about trifles like the odd cobweb of paw-marked upholstery until the next session. But Nigel, my exquisite London crony, had to be different – he had to visit between duly authorised entertaining dates, which meant that I had to do a special clean-up just for him. I worked myself into a frenzy, cleaning, washing, scrubbing and polishing. I knew that if he found so much as a speck of dust (and you can bet your life that if there was a speck to be found, he would find it) he would immediately have an attack of the vapours, murmuring feebly about his allergy, his chest, his delicate constitution. As my own constitution was a bit on the fragile side when it came to coping with one of his turns, I wasn't taking any chances. By the time he was due to arrive the cottage positively sparkled; I, on the other hand, looked as though I'd been put through the wringer. Still, I wasn't the one on display.

Terrified of disarranging anything or leaving a trace of ash anywhere, I took myself, my cats, my ciggies and, as an afterthought, my vodka outside to await the Arrival. The car drew up and Nigel got out and leaned languidly against the bonnet for a moment or two so that I could get the full effect. He had abandoned the deerstalker cap and tweed cape in favour of the Impoverished Gentry look – green wellies, corduroy breeches and hacking jacket. Moss Bros. must be doing very nicely out of his visits, I reflected; I wonder if they'll give me a commission? He picked his way delicately through the mud to the cottage door and I ushered him into the living room. Everything looked beautiful and I stood back and awaited his reaction. It wasn't quite what I expected. He gave a carefully modulated scream then subsided in a limp and exquisitely choreographed heap against the wall, fanning his brow with a pure silk, expensively perfumed handkerchief. Shocked, I followed his gaze and there, right bang in the middle of the floor, was a small, very dead shrew. One of the cats, with meticulous but ill-judged timing, had very thoughtfully provided a 'welcome' present. (Thinking about it later, I decided that more likely the cats couldn't stand the unaccustomed tidiness of the cottage and had left the shrew there to provide a homely touch.) I led Nigel to a chair and plied him with restorative draughts of brandy. After the second or third dose the colour returned to his cheeks and his eyelids fluttered open. He looked at me steadily for a moment or two and then said in a carefully controlled voice, 'My dear Sylvia, I know you love animals; we all love animals. Some of us even have pets. But not pet rodents, my sweet. And certainly not *dead* pet rodents!'

Casual callers have to take things very much as they find them. Sometimes I get lucky and spot potential visitors coming up the path, which gives me a few minutes to throw things into cupboards, turn cushions round to show the clean side and hide the cats' toys under the sofa. But if ever I find myself getting all steamed up trying to cope with unscheduled visitors I think back to the Day of the Dog and am immediately consoled. Because I know that nothing can ever again be as bad as that. I answered a knock at the door and was confronted by a woman who looked vaguely familiar, a man, a toddler, a baby in a carricot, several bags of baby requisites and a large black dog of uncertain ancestry. I must have looked a bit bemused because the woman said, 'Don't you remember me? I'm Marion Lawford well you'd know me as Marion Chamber that was before I got married to Len, this is Len, Len Lawford, my husband, and this is Mickey and the baby is Ellen and we happened to run into Sally the other day, you remember Sally she used to be Sally Hopkins she's Sally Clarke now she married Robin Clarke you remember Robin . . .' By now my head was spinning and I was searching desperately among the names she was dropping like confetti for a clue, any clue, to the identity of this very chatty lady. Meanwhile the voice was chuntering on: '. . . gave us your address and we thought well it's a nice day why not have a drive out in the country and call on Sylvia so here we are and if you can just give me a hand in with the baby's things. . . ' I gave up and herded them inside.

'Pussycat!' yelled Mickey, making a grab for Char-

91

lie's tail. Charlie, usually very sociable, remembered all the important things he had to do outside and made a dash for the door, closely followed by the rest of the cats. Thwarted, Mickey lashed out with his foot and kicked the dog who started barking furiously, waking up the baby who immediately added her 300 decibels to the already unbearable noise level. 'I'll make tea,' I gasped, wanting nothing so much as to join the cats and escape outside. The dog followed me into the kitchen, getting under my feet and tripping me up every time I turned round. When I opened the fridge to get out the milk his face lit up and, shoving me aside with a well-aimed butt from his rock-solid head, he grabbed the first thing that came to hand – my supper chops. In a daze, I watched as he took the chops into the living room and settled down to eat them on the carpet. I waited for Marion to do something or say something, anything. Eventually she did. 'Well, he's certainly enjoying that, isn't he? Chops! You are a lucky doggie!' I bit my tongue – visitors' dogs, like visitors' children, have to be accepted, warts and all, just like the visitors themselves. But I did think one of them might have made some attempt to control the dog.

I brought in the tea tray and set it down on the table. 'Would you be a love and warm the baby's feed?' asked Marion, handing me a bottle. Gritting my teeth I went out to the kitchen and put a saucepan of water on the stove. Suddenly there was an almightly crash from the living room. I flew in, took one look and clamped my eyes tightly shut. It's all a dream, I told myself, when you open them you'll find it never happened. Very cautiously I prised my eyes open. It was no dream. The teapot, the milk jug, the sugar, the cups and plates, the cakes, everything was scattered all over the floor in a sticky liquid goo. The dog was licking the cakes and

Mickey was gnawing on the now-abandoned chop bones. The silence was so electric that I could almost feel it crackle. Then Marion said defensively, 'It was an accident. The dog, he knocked over the table.' I bared my teeth in the nearest thing I could manage to a smile and hissed, 'Not to worry. We'll soon get it cleaned up,' and set to work with dustpan, brush and mop to clear the debris, watched by an apparently unconcerned Marion and her equally unconcerned spouse. 'Is the baby's feed ready?' she enquired brightly. Oh Lord, I'd forgotten all about it. I rushed into the kitchen and was met by a pall of smoke – the water had boiled away, leaving the saucepan a blackened twisted mess of burnt metal. Without thinking I grabbed the saucepan, gave a yell of agony and sent it flying across the kitchen; it landed on the few unbroken crocks that I had salvaged from the holocaust and reduced the lot to rubble. Over the next five minutes the smoke-blackened air turned blue as I systematically worked my way through my entire vocabulary of cuss-words. I was surprised at the range of my repertoire and so, I suspect, were Marion and Len, if their faces were anything to go by.

The visit dragged on and so did Marion's voice – non-stop. Dear God, will they never go? I pleaded, my face throbbing from the strain of smiling at Mickey as he uprooted all the plants from their pots and, using the teacups as 'buckets', made sand-pies with the compost. 'Who's a naughty boy, then?' giggled Marion roguishly, then to me 'He's ever so good with his hands, really creative, so we don't like to discourage him.' *Discourage* him? It was as much as I could do not to clobber him. Still smiling through clenched teeth, I watched as their dog methodically shredded the fireside rug to spaghetti and then, as the wool from the rug met up with the previously consumed chops and cakes in his stomach, threw up the lot all over the sofa. 'Well, better out than in, I always say,' chirped Marion. I'll bet you do, I thought murderously. After what seemed like an eternity I saw Marion and Len exchanging glances and then she uttered the most wonderful words I had heard all day. 'I think we'd better be going, it's a long journey and the kids get a big fractious if they miss their bedtime and what with all the excitement they probably won't get to sleep anyway . . .' I let her prattle on – after the magic word 'going' I wasn't really taking anything in.

They all piled into the car while I unceremoniously threw coats, teddy-bears, nappies (used and unused), towels, bottles and heaven only knows what else in after them. I wanted nothing so much as to see the back of them. Len started up the car and I began the count-down to actual depature . . . Ten, nine, eight . . . 'My ball,' yelled Mickey, 'I forgot my ball!' 'I'll get it,' I cried, terrified that they might all get out again to search for it. I dashed inside, grabbed the ball, and was just about to dash out again when I noticed the dog fast asleep on the sofa. Dear God, I thought, yanking him off, if it hadn't been for Mickey's blasted ball they'd have gone without him. I hauled him outside and called, 'You forgot something else – your dog!' They all gaped at me, open-mouthed. Then Len uttered the first words to pass his lips all day. 'Our dog? We thought he was yours! He was sitting on the step when we came.' Oh God, I pleaded, just get me through the rest of this unbelievable day and I'll never ask You for anything again. The Lawfords drove off with promises to come again (You just try it, I thought darkly) and I was left holding an exceeding smug-looking dog. I wondered if he made a habit of this sort of thing, attaching himself to complete strangers and using them as entre to

94

tea-parties. I could find no name or address on his collar, but he was obviously well-fed and well-cared for. Why wouldn't he be? I thought, living the life of Riley at the expense of mugs like me. I released my hold and he trotted off across the fields with the air of a chap who had things to do and places to go. Probably going home to have another supper, I thought bitterly, remembering my own chopless supper. It wasn't until much later, when I was sitting by the fire and revelling in the beautiful peace and quiet, that it struck me that I still didn't known who the hell Marion was!

During school holidays there is a constant stream of children knocking on the door for drinks of water, bits of string, bags for their conkers or just a chat. I soon realised that these were just excuses – what they really wanted was to see the animals and birds. I encouraged them in this, thinking that if they got to know and identify with animals while they were young, they would be less likely to ill-treat and brutalise them when they were older. As so often happens with well-intentioned schemes, it sometimes backfired. During one school holiday the paddock gate was left open and the donkeys got out. I appealed to some passing youngsters to give me a hand catching them. With whoops of delight they chased after the donkeys, yelling 'Ride 'em cowboy!' and thrashing around with ropes and sticks, with the not unexpected result that the donkeys immediately stampeded and took off in all directions. So instead of them all ending up at the same farm and offending one farmer, they finished up at four different farms, thereby upsetting four farmers. Still, the youngsters meant well and what they lacked in donkey-catching expertise they certainly made up for in enthusiasm. I thanked them for their 'help' and gave them 50 pence each.

Twenty minutes later I was looking out of an upstairs window when I saw them holding open the paddock gate and courteously waving the donkeys through into Graham Christie's field. Furious I went galloping downstairs and rushed outside, practically colliding with the lads who, wearing angelic expressions informed me: 'Your donkeys are out again. Would you like us to help you catch them?' Biting back the scream that was fighting to get out and clasping my hands behind my back in case I did them an inadvertent mischief, I said with icy politeness, 'What a good idea. As you were the ones who so kindly let them out it seems only fair that you should have the privilege of getting them back again.' The trouble is that I just can't afford to antagonise these youngsters. Just as people who live in glasshouses shouldn't throw stones, so people who live in isolated positions shouldn't make enemies – not if they don't want to wake up one morning and find their barn burnt down, their birds slaughtered and their donkeys gone.

There was one gang of about seven 11 to 12 year olds who spent practically every day of the Easter holidays hanging around the paddock, shouting and skylarking and frightening the donkeys. When I asked them, very politely, to leave I was invited to bog off. There seemed no point in forcing the issue – I couldn't make them go if they didn't want to and threats to call the police might solve the immediate problem but would very likely call down retribution in the long term. I said, 'All right, stay if you want to but please don't shout as it upsets the donkeys.' They looked surprised – how could shouting upset them? I explained that some of the donkeys came from unhappy homes where they had been beaten and starved and it took very little to frighten them. A wave of comprehension passed over their faces and I got the impression that some of them knew all about unhappy home lives. They asked me questions about the donkeys – where did I get them, what did they eat, did I ride them? After about half an hour they left amicably, with promises to see that 'Nobody don't hurt them donkeys; if we catch 'em at it we'll cut 'em up.' Ah, well, I thought, if you can't beat 'em, join 'em! The next day the boys were back, knocking on the door, 'Is it all right to give the donkeys crisps? We bought them specially.' I said yes, they'd be delighted, and watched their faces light up. On an impulse I told them that it was my birthday next week, would they like to come for a bit of a nosh-up? They accepted with enthusiasm, 'and we'll bring you a present.' 'No, please don't,' I begged them, my imagination working overtime as I visualised them wandering around Woolworth's, stuffing their pockets full of ill-gotten goodies: 'The defendant had set herself up as a modern-day Fagin, m'lud. Her cottage was like Aladdin's Cave, stuffed to the rafters with trinkets and knick-knacks which she had prevailed upon these poor, innocent lads to steal for her.' No thanks!

They arrived on the appointed day, all spruced up and glowing from the unaccustomed contact with soap and water. The gang leader thrust a small cardboard box into my hand: 'We know you like animals and things so we brought you this.' Oh God, I thought, listening to the soft scrabbling noises coming from the box and shuffling wildly through the possibilities. Tarantula? Rattlesnake? Death-watch beetle? Full of foreboding I opened the box and was horrified to see two baby coots inside. I knew there was no way I could keep these tiny scraps alive – they couldn't have been more than a day or two old. Struggling to keep my voice level I asked, Where did you find these birds?' They

exchanged furtive glances then one of them said, 'On the path in the woods, miss. They must have fallen out of their nest'. This was patently untrue but I knew if I upset them I'd never find out where these babies had come from. Choosing my words carefully. I said, 'I don't think they fell out of their nest because the nest would be by the water and there is no water anywhere near the path. I think probably some children who don't know any better took them from their nest and left them on the path. It was very lucky that you happened to find them, otherwise they would have died. But it we don't get them back to the mother quickly they'll die anyway. You all know the woods better than I do, perhaps you could show me the most likely place where the nest would be?'

They'll never fall for it, I thought. I watched as they looked at each other, then at their feet, then at the wall but never once at me. The silence lengthened and I was convinced that none of us would ever speak again. Then a voice piped up, 'I think I once saw some of these swimming near old man Paddick's farm.' Immediately there was a chorus of agreement: 'That's right – I saw 'em too.' 'Yeah, lots of 'em there.' 'Do you think you could show me?' I asked. 'Oh, sure – no problem. I wrapped the little ones up and tucked them back into their box and off we went. After about half an hour the boys stopped at a part of the woods I had never been to before; the river skirted the woods for about a mile and then meandered off again. There were mallards, coots, moorhens, all proudly parading their babies. 'I wonder where the nest could be?' I said idly. The boys exchanged glances. 'I think prob'ly just there' said one, pointing to a clump of reeds. 'You wait here,' I told them, and lying flat on the ground I wriggled as near to the reeds as I dared without frightening the residents. I

could just make out the mother coot's head; I un-
wrapped the babies and started to push them gently
towards her but she must have heard me – she shot up
and, with much flapping of wings and beating of the
water with her feet made it clear that I was unwelcome.
I saw five little ones in the nest and, praying that mum
couldn't count, quickly popped the orphans in with
them.

On the trek back to the cottage the boys carefully
kept off the subject of baby coots, and I didn't bring it
up again. If I hadn't already made my point the chances
were I never would. There was a slight pall over the
birthday festivities but this soon passed. Over the
months the boys continued to visit the donkeys and me,
in that order, and we established a fairly comfortable

relationship. If this were a fairy story the lads would have become reformed characters, caring for animals and leading blameless lives. And, for all I know, some of them might have done. What I do know is that some time later one of them called on me with a hard-luck story, conned his way into the cottage and stole every penny I had. The moral of this tale? I'm not sure that there is one.

CHAPTER 9

I tore the page off the calendar with a sense of disbelief –
surely it couldn't be December? Where had the year
gone? True, what with all the hoo-ha of moving into the
cottage and the comings and goings of birds and beasts
the year had been so action-packed that I'd hardly had a
chance to note the passing of the weeks and months, but
even so I couldn't believe that it was nearly Christmas.
And I hadn't bought so much as a Christmas card yet,
let alone done the thousand and one other things
associated with the festive season. Head spinning, I sat
down to make a list. I love making lists. Every room in
the cottage is littered with lists – lists of things to do,
things to buy, things to remember, urgent jobs,
not-so-urgent jobs – I even keep a list of lists! What I
like about lists is that while you're making them you're
putting off the time when you'll actually have to start
doing something about the things on them. I got out a
sheet of paper and headed it 'Christmas', then sat and
stared at it for about five minutes – where to start?

The telephone rang and I grabbed it joyfully – saved
by the bell 'Jim Barrie here,' said the disembodied
voice. 'How would you like an early Christmas present?' 'What sort of Christmas present?' I asked

cautiously. 'A badger sort,' he replied. A *badger?* Had he gone mad? In the strangled silence that ensued while I was striving desperately to find my voice he filled me in on the background. Bertie's present owner had found him as a baby after his mother had been killed and had brought him up as a pet. Now she was moving nearer to town where there were no facilities for keeping badgers, pet or otherwise, and had asked Jim to find him a good home. (Odd how it's always a 'good home' – surely no-one would ever want to find a bad home?) Anyway, he had immediately thought of me.  Bertie was absolutely no trouble, he assured me – he slept all day and only became active at night when the rest of the world, or most of it, was asleep. He'd need a large enclosure with separate sleeping quarters and if it was all right with me he'd be arriving on Wednesday. I looked at the calendar – today was Sunday. 'Yes, that'll be fine,' I said and put down the phone.

In a daze I went over to the table, crossed 'Christmas' off the top of the list and inserted 'Badger'. Underneath I wrote Enclosure, Sleeping quarters, Hay, Dishes, Food – FOOD! What on earth did badgers eat? I flicked quickly through my book of beasts and noted that they had fairly catholic tastes, apparently eating almost anything that came their way – including I was a bit concerned to see, various smallish creatures on the hoof. Still, he'd be in his enclosure so the chickens would be safe. Why, then, did I still have this feeling of unease? *Because* he'd be in an enclosure, that's why. I couldn't come to terms with the idea of keeping a fit, healthy animal shut up for the rest of its life. True, it was the only life that Bertie had ever known, but I don't honestly believe that what you've never had you never miss. Surely the urge to be free must be inherent in all wild creatures? Oh, be sensible, I told myself, he's not equipped for freedom, he doesn't know how to look after himself, he wouldn't last five minutes in the wild – in fact, all the arguments I had used on Droopy-Boobs. Yes, but I was talking about sick and injured creatures then, not a hale and hearty, fighting-fit badger. Well, there was no point in tossing arguments to and fro – the first priority was to get his accommodation ready. Fortunately this was the slack period for orphans and casualties and there was a vacant enclosure. I lined a tea chest with hay and put it in the far corner of the enclosure, so that any disturbance during the day would be minimal. Well-pleased with my efforts I went back into the cottage and made another list 'Shopping for Bertie' – honey, raisins, treacle, nuts, etc. The etcetera would cover anything else I came across that seemed to have badger acceptable properties. And while I was out I could get my Christmas cards.

By the time Jim and Bertie arrived everything was prepared and I was in a twitter of anticipation. Jim inspected the badger emporium and pronounced it satisfactory. Now for the moment I was waiting for – the introductions. These turned out to be a bit one-sided as one of the participants slept soundly through-out the proceedings. From time to time he sighed softly and twitched his whiskers before settling back into deeper slumber. He really was quite enchanting, even asleep. We took him over to the enclosure and installed him in his sleeping quarters. Just before dusk, on Jim's instructions, I made up a large bowl of bread and milk liberally laced with sugar and honey and topped with raisins, and took it out to Bertie. He was just waking up, stretching and yawning and scratching himself with all the self-indulgence of someone who has slept the sleep of the just. His whiskers twitched as the smell of supper tickled his nostrils and he came trundling over, aquiver with anticipation. As soon as I put the bowl down he stuck his snout in and joyfully dispatched the lot in about four slurps. 'Seconds?' I asked. 'Not half.' he whuffled.

After supper I sat on the tea chest and tickled his chin while he rubbed his head against my legs. 'You really are a poppet', I told him. He looked up and growled, 'you're not bad yourself'. I spent about two hours playing with him then, with heartfelt apologies, went back to the cottage. I felt awful leaving him alone, particularly on his first night here. I could give up another night's sleep, I mused – Mondays for house-work and, say, Thursdays for Bertie. But no, if I stayed up with him one night he'd just be that lonelier on the other nights. And in any case there were probably limits to the amount of deprivation my system could take. Sorry, Bertie, I told him, you'll just have to settle for a couple of hours association every evening. But I wished there was some way I could vary the monotony of his life and add a bit of spice to it. Suddenly it struck me – I could take him for walks in the evening! The next day I bought a stout collar and lead and as soon as he'd finished his supper I put them on him and opened the door of his enclosure. He looked up at me expectantly. 'Come on Bertie,' I said, 'walkies,' and led him out. At the magic word 'walkies', Charlie and Pudding sud-denly emerged from the shadows; Pudding took one look at Bertie, decided that perhaps a late-night walk wasn't such a good idea after all, and shot off again. But Charlie, after weighing up the pro's and cons of the situation, concluded that the presence of a large, animated liquorice allsort was a small price to pay for the delights of an unscheduled excursion, and happily tagged along with us.

Using a flashlight I picked my way cautiously across

the garden, with Bertie happily scampering on one side and Charlie on the other. Which way to go? Not across the paddock, I decided – five donkeys might prove a bit daunting for Bertie on his first night out. We settled for a sedate stroll along the path then back through the fields. Every so often Bertie would stop at a particularly enticing smell and snuffle excitedly for a moment or two before resuming his constitutional. After about an hour we made our way back to the enclosure and spent another hour just playing silly fools. From then on we took a walk every evening; as soon as Bertie had licked the last speck of food from his bowl he would scamper eagerly over to me and wait while I put the collar on, then scramble at the door until I opened it – OK, let's go!

In between times I tried to catch up on the pre-Christmas chores, not daring to look at the calendar and not believing what it told me when I did look. On a last-minute trip to the village I ran into Mr Sludge and on an impulse invited him up for a festive drink when he had a moment. He fished out a sludge-coloured notebook and consulted it; after pondering for a moment or two he said, 'What about next Saturday? Six o'clock if that's OK?' I said Saturday would be fine and dashed off before I found myself answering in couplets. He arrived on the dot and, as far as I could make out, wearing exactly the same clothes as he wore for work – with one exception; his hands were now encased in a pair of bright canary-yellow rubber gloves. I won't say anything, I vowed. Not a word about gloves will pass these lips.

I poured out drinks and handed him crisps and peanuts and engaged in idle chit-chat without once touching on the subject of yellow gloves. We discussed the forthcoming festival: 'I never see no rhyme or reason/For crackers in the festive season'. The weather: 'If the moon is full at Xmas/Snow will blow across from Texas.' I awarded him full marks for ingenuity – after all even the writers of Christmas card rhymes have trouble with Christmas – but none at all for credibility. And his work: 'Been in sewage all me life/That's why I never took a wife.' I was a bit confused about this – did he mean that sewage had filled his life to the exclusion of all else, or that his close association with sewage had put off prospective brides? Bit of both, probably, I decided. I saw him to the door and bade him farewell and a happy Christmas, then blurted out: 'No pink gloves today, then?' He looked affronted. 'They're my everyday gloves. I always like to dress up posh/When folks invite me for a nosh.' Serves you right, I told myself.

On Christmas Eve I recalled something I'd once read – that on the stroke of midnight donkeys all over the world kneel down in homage to that other donkey in Bethlehem nearly two thousand years ago. I decided to see if my donkeys knew of the legend. Just before midnight I tiptoed out and made my way over to the paddock. No sign of the donkeys in the shelter. Once my eyes became accustomed to the dark I made out five donkey-shaped shadows standing four-square on their legs, busily tucking into their hay. They probably don't know it's Christmas Eve, I thought, a bit sad that such a beautiful illusion had been shattered. It's always a mistake to put legends to the test – much better to accept the fact that it's because they cannot be scientifically proved that they have become legends.

While I was out I decided to go and have a chat with Bertie. I went over to his enclosure and flashed the torch, no response. Indeed, as closer inspection revealed, no Bertie. Sick with apprehension I went inside and searched every inch of the closure and his sleeping box, knowing that I was wasting my time. An animal the size of a badger wasn't likely to be hiding in a three-inch gap. But I didn's see how he could have got out – the door had been securely shut and there was no gap anywhere in the netting. I spent most of the night searching for him; I knew it was a lost cause but I had to do something and it would have been pointless going to bed as I knew I wouldn't sleep. It wasn't the fact that he'd escaped that bothered me; what really worried me was whether he could survive in the harsh world outside. Would he be able to find his own food? How would he cope with foxes? What if he was spotted by a farmer and shot? I knew there were badgers in the woods but I didn't imagine for one moment that they would put out the welcome mat for Bertie – much more likely that they'd attack him. Just before dawn I went inside for a bath and a cup of tea, then went about the daily business of letting the poultry out and feeding and watering the resident birds and beasts. 'Merry Christmas all,' I wished them dolefully and, to the birds, 'Be thankful you're not turkeys.' As I passed Bertie's enclosure I looked in one last time – and there he was, curled up fast asleep in his tea-chest! My heart lifted – it was going to be a happy Christmas after all!

After that I checked on him every night before I went to bed and his enclosure was always empty, but Cinderella-like he was always back by daylight. It occurred to me that these escapades had very likely been going on ever since he came and it was just sheer chance that I had found out. But I still had no idea how he was getting out. I waited for a full moon and after our nightly walk (though why I still bothered with these walks heaven only knows, as quite clearly Bertie was getting all the recreation and exercise he needed without any help from me) I wished him good night as usual then, instead of going inside, crept sneakily around to the back of his enclosure and prepared for a long, lonely and exceedingly cold vigil. As it turned out, it wasn't all that long. After about five minutes there was a scratching sound and I saw that Bertie was pulling up a piece of loose netting at the side of his enclosure; he then squeezed under it and, to my utter disbelief, carefully patted it down again. No wonder my investigations hadn't revealed his escape route – he was covering his tracks! I watched as he busily whiffled his way across the field adjoining the paddock and disappeared into the woods.

Next morning I was up well before dawn and waiting for him when he returned from his night on the tiles. He looked a bit surprised to see me but there was no suggestion of shame or guilt about him; on the contrary he looked insufferably pleased with himself. He snuffled at my hand and rubbed his head against my legs, but I wasn't going to be won over by any old soft soap. 'And where do you think you've been till this hour of the morning?' I asked him. 'Anyone would think you didn't have a home to go to. This is a respectable house, I'll have you know, and what the neighbours will say I shudder to think.' With the air of a man with a secret which he's keeping to himself he gave me a knowing look, ambled into his sleeping quarters and after an almighty stretch, curled up in a ball and was asleep in a trice. After thinking about it for some time, and making discreet enquiries among my neighbours to find out whether there had been any depredations among their stock (there hadn't been) I decided not to block up his escape route. He wasn't doing any harm and had apparently found a way of life that suited him – who was I to interfere?

Things went on like this for about two months and then he started missing a day every so often, not coming back until supper-time. We still took our evening walks but I had the impression that Bertie came on them more to humour me than anything else. Soon the intervals between his returns grew longer until he was using the place as a restaurant rather than as a home, coming back only for a meal and a bit of a tickle. By spring he had stopped coming back altogether, although I frequently spotted him at the edge of the woods, waiting hopefully. Here we go again, I sighed, setting up a meals-on-wheels service for him, much to his gratification. Not that he needed a home delivery service, as he was quite obviously foraging successfully for himself. But I didn't want to lose all contact with him.

CHAPTER 10

Every season here brings its own special delights, but spring is my favourite. Everything is fresh and new and full of promise, almost like a re-birth. But this spring was especially memorable because it brought into my life one of the most delightful, enchanting, lovable creatures ever to come my way. It started, like so many of the happy episodes in my new life, with a phone call from Jim Barry; how did I feel about taking in a baby tawny owl? How did I feel about it? I searched for a suitable word, couldn't find one and settled for ecstatic. After putting down the phone I just sat in a daze. I don't know what it is about owls, whether it's their cottage-loaf shape or those incredible all-seeing eyes or their haunting, soul-searing call cutting across the otherwise silent night, but to me they are the most fascinating and appealing of all birds.

The Day of the Owl duly arrived and Jim handed me a cardboard box containing what looked like a couple of amorphous blobs loosely joined together and covered in a greyish-white downy fluff which created a minor snowstorm with every movement. In the middle of the upper blob were two enormous eyes which met my gaze and held it steadily and unwinkingly, without a trace of

fear. Jim told me that the owl had fallen out of its nest and damaged both wings quite badly and would never be able to do more than just flutter about. Which meant that I could integrate him into the household without having to worry about jeopardising his chances of survival in the wild, as he could never be released. Not that it would have made a scrap of difference anyway, as it turned out, because Wol took it for granted from the word go, not so much that he belonged to the household but rather that the household belonged to him. He also made it clear that I could forget whatever I knew, or thought I knew, about owls because he was no Ordinary Owl. He was a Character. For a bundle of fluff the size of a tennis ball his cheek was astounding.

Thinking that his box probably represented some sort of security to him I left him in it that first evening. For a while all was quiet, then . . . 'scrabble, scrabble,' followed by a few minutes silence and then, more

insistently, 'scrabble, scrabble, scratch'. I watched in amazement as the box, apparently under its own steam, started perambulating across the floor. It came to an abrupt halt and then, after a bit more furious scrabbling, a fluffy head suddenly appeared; a quick lookround to get the lie of the land and then the rest of Wol emerged. Twittering crossly about the insensitivity of people who leave baby owls all alone in cardboard boxes while they are out and about enjoying themselves, he set off on a tour of the living room. I held my breath as he bustled self-importantly over to Charlie, who was asleep on the rug and, head cocked, chirrupped chattily about two inches from his ear. Charlie took this intrusion into his privacy with his customary good nature; he opened one eye, fixed Wol with an incurious stare and promptly went back to sleep. 'What, no wash?' I enquired of Charlie, knowing his compulsion to lick every newcomer into a stupor. He opened the other eye: 'What, with all that loose fluff? Do you want me to get fur balls? And in any case, have you taken a look at that beak? No thank you.' Meanwhile, Wol was getting increasingly frustrated; this furry non-owl was right in his path and it wouldn't move. Only one thing for it; giving a reasonable impersonation of an Indian fakir walking on broken glass he very carefully picked his way across Charlie, up one side and down the other. Of course he could have walked round Charlie but I soon learned that this just wasn't his way. Charlie, to his everlasting credit, didn't so much as twitch a whisker at this diabolical liberty-taking.

Wol continued on his way, much to Pudding's alarm. Because the next obstacle in his path was the chair Pudding was sitting in. He watched, transfixed with fear, as this ball of fluff came nearer and nearer. Wol came to a halt, fixed Pudding with an unwinking eye and promptly started climbing up the chair-leg. With a shriek guaranteed to raise the dead, Pudding shot off the chair, across the room and out through the cat-flap. Not in the least perturbed by this extraordinary behaviour, Wol settled himself comfortably in the Pudding-warmed seat, fluffed out his downy feathers and chirruped happily. After about five minutes he was ready to resume his tour. He hopped off the chair and picked up where he left off. When he reached the sofa, where I was sitting, he made a sharp right turn and continued straight up my leg and on to my lap. Flapping his wings furiously and coating me liberally with soft grey fluff, he settled down and cocked an enquiring eye at me. I started stroking his head and with each stroke it tilted farther and farther back until eventually he was looking at his tail. Or would have been if his eyes were open. To my astonishment, I realised that he was in a near-hypnotic trance. I stopped stroking and one eye snapped open, fixing me with a look which said quite distinctly, 'Keep going – it's lovely!'

An unwritten law of this establishment is that whoever has possession of a chair is entitled to keep it. I don't know who introduced this law, certainly not me as it usually turns out that I'm the one who ends up on the floor. Anyway, Wol soon put an end to all that. If he wanted a particular chair then, cat-occupied or not, he is going to have it. With Minnie and Pudding a long, meaningful gaze is enough – unnerved, they are off like a shot. But Charlie is made of sterner stuff – no bug-eyed feather duster is going to deprive him of his chair. After giving Charlie the full treatment (fixed gaze, flapping wings and exasperated chittering) a few times, to no avail, Wol decided that more direct measures were called for. Giving no indication that he is

113

even aware of Charlie's presence he climbs up the chair-leg and settles himself cosily alongside him. Charlie had absolutely no intention of sharing a chair with this pushy upstart but to give in immediately would be infra dig. With a languid stretch and an air of studied unconcern which is patently meant to convey that he was going anyway, he slides gracefully to the floor.

Strangely enough, the only exception Wol made to this your-chair-is-my-chair business was Rufus. Rufus had become a bit techy in his old age and, no longer able to fight for what he wanted, resorted to martyrdom and the old guilt routine to achieve his ends. I don't know whether it was out of respect for Rufus's advanced years or a disinclination to be on the receiving end of his I-did-think-that-in-my-declining-years-I-might-be-allowed-to-sleep-in-peace act, but Wol never attempted to oust Rufus from his chair. Characteristically, Rufus interpreted this as a slight – Not only do I not count around here, I am also invisible, I don't exist.

Owls, of course, are nocturnal but Wol saw no point in staying up at night when there was nobody to play with and then sleeping the day away and missing all the fun. So he promptly reversed the process and took to keeping people hours. But there is not doubt that he is friskiest at night. Most of the day he sits on his perch by the French windows, keeping a benevolent eye on the world around him. Occasionally he takes a cat-nap, but always with one eye open just in case he should miss anything. Round about eight o'clock he starts perking up. Following a feather-by-feather preening session to ensure that he is properly turned out for the evening's activities, he hops onto my shoulder and chirrups happily in my ear, telling me all about his day. This goes on for about three minutes until he suddenly

114

catches sight of my hair and, apparently appalled at the condition of my plumage, gives it a thorough going-over with his beak. After about five minutes he stands back and views his handiwork with a critical eye. A hasty glance in the mirror and I see that I am apparently wearing a pot-scraper on my head. Wol, however, seems well-pleased with the results of his labour and nods approvingly. He hops on to the back of the sofa and looks around for 'his' mouse. Actually, it is the cats' mouse but on the basis of what yours is mine, Wol has assumed sole proprietorship, much to the cats' disgust. I bought them a new mouse, which they immediately rejected on the grounds that it lacked the battered familiarity of the old one. Without much hope I offered it to Wol in exchange for the one he had stolen; still clutching his ill-gotten trophy he took the new mouse delicately in his beak and, with the utmost contempt, dropped it on the floor.

The sofa-back is one of Wol's favourite parking spots, particularly if I am sitting on the sofa. Of course playing with a catnip mouse is fun, but it's even more fun if you can keep dropping it on someone's head and then chitter in their ear until they give it back to you so that you can drop it on their head again . . . and so on, and on, and on . . . Five minutes of this and my head is beginning to throb so I confiscate the mouse. Wol reacts exactly like a baby who's had his lollipop taken away; he screams, he jumps up and down with rage, he swears at me. I ignore this shocking behaviour; Wols, like children must learn that they cannot always have things their own way. Seeing that his temper tantrum is getting him nowhere, he changes tack. He switches off the sound (oh, joy!) and stalks huffily to the far end of the sofa. Turning his back on me, he sits and studies the wall. The message is clear – Wol is sulking. I take no notice. I know, and he knows, that he won't be able to keep it up for long. Two or three minutes pass and then I become aware of a tweaking sensation in my scalp; Wol is trying to attract my attention by pulling my hair out – one hair at a time. I put my hand up to my head and his talons close around my finger; with the utmost delicacy he picks it up and, holding it like a hot-dog, gently nibbles it. Having seen that beak reduce a lump of beef to mincemeat in a matter of seconds, I appreciate his restraint.

Like most of us, Wol has his moods. There are times when he wants to socialise and there are other times when he wants to be left strictly alone. Fair enough. The trouble is that when Wol is feeling sociable, *everybody* has to be sociable. Unfortunately his peaks come at night, just when I am beginning to wind down. My idea of relaxation after a hard day is to settle down with a not-too-demanding book. Wol, not being much of a reader himself, can't understand what I see in books. He hops on to my lap to investigate what it is that I find so much more engrossing than his company. He inspects the book and spots its potential immediately. Grabbing a page in his beak, he produces instant confetti. After a couple of fraught interviews with the librarian, watching her eyebrows disappearing into her hair line and her mouth curling in disbelief as I tried to explain that the book had been decimate by an illiterate owl, I gave up my library card. I also gave up snatching the odd forty winks by the fire. Just as I am dozing off there is a tugging at my trouser leg followed by a scrabbling sensation as Wol hauls himself on to my lap. A short hop on to my chest brings his face within two inches of mine. I open my eyes hurriedly to forestall his next move – nibbling gently at my eyelids to see if I'm in there.

Like Basil, Wol is a great one for television, but his manner of viewing is a bit unorthodox. He sits on top of the set and hangs over the front of it, so that all the images appear upside-down to him; who knows, they might look better that way. What I do know is that I find it very difficult to concentrate when the top half of the screen is obliterated by an upside-down Wol. Any new sight or sound immediately arouses his interest. The first time he heard the whirring of the fan heater his eyes widened and putting on his we-must-look-into-this expression, he trundled over to investigate. The blast of warm air stopped him in his tracks but after a few moments' pause for reflection he gingerly inched his way forward again. Another pause, followed by a further inch or two of progress. Gradually, as the warm air whiffed through his feathers, a look of joy spread over his face. He hopped onto the top of the heater and slowly shuffled backwards until his rear end was over the vent. Eyes closed in owlish bliss, he swayed gently from side to side as the warm air rippled through his tail feathers. From then on the fan heater was his number-one parking site – until the day when, having taken up his usual rump-over-vent position, it dawned on him that something was missing – no warm air. Clearly put out, he turned round and poked his head into the vent to see what was holding things up. No apparent obstruction – so what now? He shot me an enquiring look and, taking pity on him, I switched on the heater. Aaahh, bliss! He turned around and repositioned his tail-end over the vent.

Wol's usual method of locomotion is a lop-sided waddle, a bit like a drunken sailor with corns. But if he spots something on the floor that bears investigation, a spider for instance, he affects a mincing gait, picking his way daintly across the room on tippy-toes. After

117

much head-nodding to pinpoint his quarry he places his head on one side and rivets it, or so he thinks, with a piercing glance. More often than not the spider has gone by this time but undaunted Wol keeps his eye firmly fixed on the spot where it was. A funny thing about Wol is that he has absolutely no killer instinct, which for a bird of prey is odd indeed. Just as well that he'll never have to earn his own living as the chances are he would starve to death. He adores beetles but can't bring himself to kill them or eat them alive. If he spots one he jumps up and down in a paroxysm of excitement, screeching hysterically until I come and kill it for him. He then swallows it in one gulp. Being a bit on the squeamish side myself, this is not exactly a task I relish.

I once offered him an earthworm, thinking he would regard this as a real treat. He eyed my offering with distaste and stepped back a few paces. Of course, I thought, he's never seen a worm before so he doesn't know that it's good to eat. Carefully picking it up with tweezers (no way could I handle a worm!) I held it to his beak. He took it with the utmost delicacy and then, when it started to wriggle, dropped it in horror. He watched its contortions on the floor for a moment or two then, with exaggerated fastidiousness, picked it up and took a tentative nibble before dropping it back on the floor. By this time I had had enough, and so I imagine had the worm. Just as I was about to tweezer it away there was a sudden movement and the worm was gone. Thomas, my resident toad, had obviously been watching this pantomime from his flower pot; fed up with the shilly-shallying over the worm he took matters into his own hands and, with one quick gulp, put an end to the whole wretched business. It all happened so quickly that Wol couldn't take it in. His face wrinkled with puzzlement, he looked from the floor to me and back

118

to the floor again. 'But there was a worm there,' he chittered plaintively, 'I know there was.'

Owls are meat-eaters and Wol has chicken, beef, rabbit, heart and, if he's very lucky, the occasional dead mouse brought in by one of the cats. This doesn't happen very often as the cats are no great shakes as hunters. But Wol has an enormous fan club and from time to time one of his admirers calls bearing gifts in the shape of dead mice, voles and even the occasional rat. Wol adores mice; the odd one that comes his way is regarded as a rare delicacy. None of this gulping it down in one go as he does with chicken or beef; each mouthful is savoured and relished. It really is quite disgusting. After mice, Wols favourite food is whatever I happen to be eating. Immediately I sit down to a meal he comes bustling over, climbs up my leg and onto my shoulder, and from this vantage point monitors every bite I put into my mouth. If he spots a titbit he fancies he grabs it off the fork; anything that doesn't come up to expectations is dropped down the back of my neck.

Unlike Basil, Wol has no objections to going to bed, but he has to do it his way. 'Come on Wol, bedtime,' I say and he waddles over to the door leading to the stairway and waits for me to open it. Although he'll quite happily travel all over the place perched on my shoulder or, more usually, my head, he considers it infra dig to be carried up to bed – he insists on walking upstairs, probably because this gives him more opportunities to poodle about and put off the time when he actually has to go to bed. Three hops up, then a pause to see if I'm following. I make encouraging noises, whereupon he trips down to the bottom again, passing me en route. Intrigued by this turn of events he hops back up, keeping three steps ahead of me until he reaches the top. He then turns and waits for me,

119

punctuating every step I take with an enthusiastic nod of the head. Immediately I reach the top he gives a squawk of delight and hoppity-hops down to the bottom again. This ritual has to be repeated three times, then he is ready for bed. Well, almost. First he has to climb the Venetian blind in the study and go through his Tarzan routine, swinging from the cord. Then a security check on the wastepaper basket to make sure that nothing of value has been thrown away. Every piece of paper is taken out, studied closely then minutely shredded. He then looks around to see what other time-wasting activity he can indulge in; catching my eye and noting the steely glint in it, it occurs to him that he's pushing his luck. With a sigh of resignation he graciously allows himself to be picked up and put to bed.

Wol had only been with me a few weeks and already I couldn't imagine a life without him. 'Oh Wol,' I told him, 'we're going to have a lovely summer. We'll stay out in the garden all day and you can help me with the chores and get to know all the other residents. Won't that be fun?' He turned his enormous eyes on me: 'You do go on, don't you?'

CHAPTER 11

Sadly, the spring that brought Wol also brought tragedy. For some reason now I had noticed that Rufus was withdrawing more and more into himself, showing very little interest in what was going on around him and just wanting to be left along to live out what time was left to him in peace. Although he was still eating well he became very thin and I called the vet, thinking that it might be kindest to have him put down. After an exhaustive examination Mr Partridge told me that Rufus was not suffering from any specific disease, all his symptoms were part of the ageing process – something that would come to all of us one day, 'if we're lucky.' He assured me that Rufus was in no pain and, although his life was clearly coming to an end, there was no reason why he shouldn't live out the rest of it in a familiar, love-filled home and let nature take its course. If at any time I suspected that Rufus was suffering or in pain then he would come out immediately and bring it to a merciful end.

For the next two weeks there was no change in Rufus; he spent all day sleeping in his chair, going outside only for essential purposes (he refused to use a litter tray), and coming straight back in again. And then

one morning he suddenly awoke with a start and went over to the kitchen door. He didn't use the cat-flap but stood there, miaowing insistently until I opened the door. I watched as he slowly made his way around the garden, visiting all his old haunts – the compost heap, the apple tree, even the caravan. Mission completed, he came back to the kitchen door and lay down just outside. I left the door open so that I could keep an eye on him but he made no attempt to come inside. After about twenty minutes it started to rain, so I picked him up and put him in his chair, but he wouldn't settle until I let him out again. I got a large cardboard box and put it outside and he crawled into it, with just his head out in the soft spring rain. I stayed with him and watched as he sank quietly into his last sleep, then buried him under the apple tree. My tears were for myself; Rufus had enjoyed a long, happy life and when the time came to die he had done so with dignity and in the way he wanted. But the gap he left was appalling; he had been with me for so long that I couldn't remember a life without him.

But nature abhors a vacuum and if she sees a gap usually sends something along to fill it. So when Monty rang a few days later and asked if I would like a dog, I was convinced that it was fate; the dog was nature's gap-filler. My faith wavered a bit when he told me that it was an Old English Sheepdog – the gap wasn't *that* big – but quickly reasserted itself. After all, we were talking about emotional gaps, and the emotional gap left by Rufus's death was immeasurable. Just the same, I thought it advisable to build in a few safeguards, just in case – fate has been known to play the occasional practical joke. I said I would take the dog 'on approval' for two weeks. If, by the end of that time, things were not working out it would go back to its present owners. I hated the idea of shoving the dog around from pillar to post, but having tried twice before to introduce a dog into the household, with the result that all the cats left home, it was the best I could do. Monty told me that Bubbles (*Bubbles?*) belonged to the daughter of an acquaintance who was expecting a baby and felt that her present London flat was too small to accommodate them all. A surge of fury swept over me at the imbecility of people who buy large dogs to keep in a town flat. The fact that they usually get them as puppies and don't realise just what they have taken on until the dog is fully grown just makes it worse, to my mind, because it shows that they have given no more consideration to the purchase than they would to a loaf of bread. Still, it wasn't for me to make moral judgements.

Came the appointed day and a car containing four adults, two children, several large sacks of canine requisites and one Old English Sheepdog drew up and disgorged its contents on my doorstep. Bubbles' coat I was sorry to see, had been shorn practically to skin level and her tail had been docked. 'Come, Bubbles, meet your new mummy,' said Bubbles' old mummy leading her over to me. Bubbles drew back, bared her teeth and snarled at me. Well, that's a good start, I thought, thankful that I had inserted a let-out clause in the contract. True, my original reservations had been concerned with a potential canine–feline incompatability – the possibility that Bubbles might not take to me hadn't crossed my mind. I suppose we all need the occasional blow to the ego from time to time, if only to keep us in touch with the realities of life. Eunice, Bubbles' owner, assured me that there was nothing personal in Bubbles' behaviour, she always snarled at strangers; that's what made her such a splendid guard dog. The chorus of agreement that arose from the rest of the family, far from allaying my anxiety, just made it worse. They were trying too hard.

We all went inside for a cup of tea and were almost sent flying by three animated bundles of fur who, after one look at Bubbles, were off to see a man about a mouse. Wol, favoured Bubbles with a cursory glance, decided that she wasn't edible, and went back to contemplating his navel. Suddenly there was a piercing shriek from Eunice, 'It's alive,' she squealed, pointing to Wol, 'I thought it was stuffed!' I remarked drily that I was not in the habit of stuffing members of the family. During tea Eunice and Bill filled me in on Bubbles' requirements and my initial wave of anger abated somewhat, because it was quite clear that they were all devoted to her. Yet in a way that made it worse; if they had given a bit of thought to the future before buying her they wouldn't now be in the heartbreaking position of trying to find a new home for her.

They unpacked her folding bed, sleeping blanket, bath, feeding bowls, brushes and combs, flea powder, worm tablets, vitamin pills and tins of dog food and, to my amazement, her pedigree. Studying her immaculate bloodline I wasn't surprised that she'd snarled at me – I certainly wasn't in her class! Feeding, they assured me, was no problem – she would eat literally anything, even scraps. All the time we were talking Bubbles was watching Eunice and Bill like a hawk; every time one of them made a move she was after them like a shot. I got the distinct impression that she had been through this business many times before and my heart ached for her. Here were the people she had loved and trusted since puppyhood, and whom she would have followed to the ends of the earth, cold-bloodedly leaving her with people she didn't know and, if her reaction to me was typical, didn't much like. The hurt and bewilderment must have been unbearable. Which brought us to the question that was on all our minds – how were they going to get away without her noticing? My original idea was that I would take Bubbles for a walk and when we got back they would be gone. But that was before I met Bubbles and realised that she would probably welcome death and torture as an alternative to going anywhere with me. Eventually we decided that they would leave one by one; when only Eunice was left she would take Bubbles out into the kitchen and feed her and, while she was eating, Eunice would sneak out. None of us was naive enough to think that this was the ideal solution, but in the absence of any other it would have to do. It might have worked better if each of the departing guests had just got up and left quietly, but none of them could bear to go without bidding Bubbles an emotional goodbye. Sinking to their knees they clasped her around the neck and sobbed remorsefully in

125

her ear, thereby ensuring that if she hadn't realised what was going on before she certainly did now. As the first one left she set up a mournful howling that made my scalp prickle and which increased in intensity with each subsequent departure.

At last only Eunice was left and Bubbles was going to make darned sure that she didn't go anywhere without her. She followed Eunice into the kitchen and watched as she opened a tin of food and emptied it into her dish, but no way was she going to eat it – what, and take her eyes off Eunice? No fear! In the end I went outside and got one of the children to call Bubbles through the window: while she was distracted, Eunice made her getaway through the kitchen door. Realising that she'd been conned and unwilling to believe that her beloved family could be responsible, Bubbles came to the only possible conclusion in the circumstances – it was all my fault. So she bit me. This was a bit unexpected but I couldn't find it in my heart to blame her – in her place I'd probably have done the same. Thinking that she'd feel happier, or at any rate, less miserable with familiar things around her, I went over to get her blanket. The next thing I knew I was hurled to the ground by about three-and-a-half hundredweight or raging sheepdog, the blanket was torn from my hand and my wrist was being gnawed in a very business-like manner by a set of extremely impressive choppers. So that's why they're called canine teeth, I thought idiotically, then pulled myself together and, with a show of courage that certainly didn't reflect how I felt, pushed her off. Because I was shocked to realise that I really was afraid of her. This will never do, I thought; if she suspects that I'm in fear of her we'll never establish any sort of relationship. Although I must admit that my hopes of ever achieving any sort of rapport with Bubbles were

126

already fading fast. I knew that her behaviour was a reflection of her misery and I longed to comfort and reassure her, but she wouldn't let me get close enough. As far as Bubbles was concerned I was The Enemy.

The days that followed were so dreadful that I still have nightmares about them. The cats immediately left home, and I didn't blame them. For two pins I'd have gone with them. Give it time, I told myself. Once Bubbles settles down and becomes part of the family the cats will come to terms with her. And they might well have done; what I hadn't bargain for was Bubbles not accepting the cats. When, after a couple of days, Charlie cautiously put his nose through the cat-flap to see if it was safe to come home again, Bubbles made a grab for him, pulled him through the flap and, to my horror, began to worry him. I got the broom handle and chased Bubbles off while Charlie fled to safety. I ran out after him and picked him up; to my relief, apart from the loss of a few tufts of fur, he was unharmed. At least, physically. Emotionally he was terribly, terribly hurt. All his life, with the exception of the inexplicable Flossie episode, he had known nothing but love; he had given love freely and indiscriminately and it had almost always been returned. Now suddenly, in his own home, he was attacked and mauled by a great mountain of a monster. He mewed piteously, 'Why did you bring that thing here? We were happy, weren't we, just you and us and the birds and the donkeys?' It was a question I was to ask myself many, many times over the next few days.

Feeding Bubbles was an absolute nightmare. I know Eunice had told me that she'd eat anything – unfortunately, Eunice forgot to tell Bubbles. She turned up her nose at all my offerings; liver, beef, heart, rabbit, chicken, tinned dog food, tinned people food – she rejected the lot. In desperation I went right through

127

the freezers, (both animal & human) taking out and defrosting everything in the hope of finding something she would eat. When I ran out of likely foods I tried unlikely ones and, to my joy and relief, finally struck gold. She was mad about pork pies. I couldn't defrost them quickly enough for her – one gulp and they were gone. I got in a further supply so that there'd be something to fall back on, but now that I knew her refusal to eat wasn't due to misery, I felt that she should have a more balanced diet – dog cannot live by pork pies alone. Bubbles disagreed – it had to be pork pies or nothing. Never one to give up without a fight I started spiking her pies with meat and rabbit, but she wasn't going to be fooled that easily. She carefully nosed out all the nourishing extras and 'buried' them under the mat.

Another problem was exercising her, as she made it quite clear that she wouldn't be seen dead anywhere with me. The minute I picked up her lead she growled and bared her teeth, just daring me to come anywhere near her with it. It's all bluff, I told myself, she's trying it on. Don't let her intimidate you, just show her who's boss. Bristling with resolve I took hold of her collar and immediately found my hand impaled on her teeth. Show her who's boss? She already knew who was boss, and so did I. Her former owners, about whom I was beginning to entertain thoughts verging on the homicidal, told me they never took her out for walks (and I could see why) but just let her out when she wanted to go: 'She always comes back all right and never gets into any trouble.' I was not at all happy about letting her out on her own, but on the other hand she had to exercise, not to mention the delicate matter of attending to her personal needs. As it turned out the question of 'letting her out' didn't arise; if she wanted to go out, she went. If it meant knocking me over or breaking down the door

128

in order to get out then she was quite prepared to do so –
and she did!

Despite all my efforts to make Bubbles feel happy
and secure, to let her know that there was all the love in
the world just waiting to be tapped if only she would
give us the chance, she showed no sign of unbending.
She decided that certain parts of the living room were
'hers' and therefore out of bounds to anyone else. Her
territory took in the area in front of the broom
cupboard, which meant that I couldn't get to any of the
household requisites; the sofa and its immediate environs, and the door leading to the kitchen. This last
posed a real problem, as there was no way I could get
into the kitchen without trespassing on her property
and getting mauled for my pains. In the end I had to go
out through the front door, walk round the cottage to
the back door and get into the kitchen that way – not a
lot of fun when it's pouring with rain. But that wasn't
the end of it – once I'd got out she frequently wouldn't
let me in again!

Sitting in the barn one cold wet morning, surrounded
by three expatriate cats and thinking about Bubbles in
sole occupancy of a warm, cosy cottage, it occurred to
me that there was something very wrong somewhere.
My ruminations were interrupted by the sound of
someone banging on the kitchen door, followed in short
order by the sound of an irate dog hurling himself
against the door inside and barking her head off.
Cautiously I poked my head out of the barn and there,
dead on cue, was the Laughing Policeman. Oh God, I
thought, that's all I need. How he always manages to
time his calls so that he catches me in an embarrassing
situation, I'll never know – probably picks up the
vibrations on his radio. With all the nonchalance I
could muster, which wasn't a lot, I walked over to him.

'Looking for me?' 'Ah, there you are,' he said, eyeing me keenly and taking in the book and cushion in one hand, the vodka and ciggies in the other and the blanket draped poncho-style over my shoulders, 'Camping out, I see. Cottage-living too civilised for you, after the caravan?' I wondered, fleetingly, what the penalty was for duffing-up a copper, decided that whatever it was it wasn't worth it and replied idiotically, 'No, just clearing out the barn.' He pondered this for a while and then remarked, 'H'mm – interesting things you keep in your barn'. How in heaven's name did I get involved in this ridiculous non-conversation, I wondered, and more to the point, how do I get out of it?

'Is this a social call,' I enquired, 'or was there something specific?' He looked disappointed, but pulling himself together and assuming his official manner said, 'I am making enquiries about the ownership and present whereabouts of a dog.' Making a conscious effort to control my face so that the sense of foreboding and dread that was welling up inside me wouldn't become apparent, I asked warily, and against a background of frantic yelping, 'What dog would that be then?' 'We've been having complaints about a very big dog that's been worrying cattle and chasing poultry,' he informed me solemnly. This time there was no way I could keep the shock and horror from showing in my face. He eyed me shrewdly and with a gesture towards the appalling din coming from inside the cottage enquired laconically, 'That it?' I nodded dumbly. 'Well, let's have a look at the miscreant,' he said chattily and, before I could unfreeze my face and stop him, he opened the kitchen door and made to go inside. The next thing he knew he was flat on his back and Bubbles was haring off across the paddock. I helped him to his feet and led him inside and, after installing him in a

130

comfortable chair, made him a cup of tea. During this time, not a word was spoken by either of us. I assume he was too winded to give voice; for my part, I couldn't think of anything to say. Knowing my talent, when I can't think of anything to say for saying all the wrong things, I judged it safer to keep quiet.

He finished his tea, stood up and gave me a 'need I say more?' look. I got the message and, as soon as he had gone, rang Eunice and told her the situation. Quite apart from all the other problems, I explained that the way Bubbles was going on, there was a more than even chance that she would be shot by an enraged farmer. Eunice didn't sound at all surprised and said that she and Bill would come and collect Bubbles that evening. The joyous welcome Bubbles gave them broke my heart particularly as I knew that she would probably have to go through this dreadful business all over again. I don't believe that her reaction to me was a personal thing; I'm convinced that she was a one-family dog and would have behaved in exactly the same way towards any other potential owner. I'm equally convinced that Eunice and Bill knew all about it and had deliberately not told me in case I had refused to have her. And they were absolutely right.

CHAPTER 12

The sense of utter relief following Bubbles' departure was overwhelming. The first day I spent just wandering around the living room, exulting in setting foot again on forbidden territory, and hopping in and out through the kitchen door for the sheer delight of doing so without let or hindrance. I would never have believed that so much joy could be derived from such simple things, and I wondered whether recidivists deliberately got caught in criminal activities and returned to prison for the sheer pleasure of experiencing the rediscovered delights of freedom when they were released. The cats returned home and apart from one or two reproachful looks, made it clear that they were prepared to forgive and forget on the understanding that such a thing was never, ever allowed to happen again. Don't worry, I assured them fervently, it won't. And, joy of joys, Wol could come out of exil. During Bubbles brief sojourn, he had been banished to the study, much to his annoyance. The way he saw it, if anyone was going to be banned from the living room it should be the loud-mouthed hearth-rug that was causing all the trouble rather than him. I entirely agreed. But I couldn't take a chance on keeping Wol downstairs while Bubbles was

132

about – who knows, she might well have regarded him as an acceptable alternative to pork pies. Settled on his old familiar perch Wol looked all around him and sighed happily. Fixing the cats with an inpenetrable stare he informed them, 'I'm back, so watch it.' 'We noticed,' they replied unenthusiastically, 'but better the devil you know . . .'

I saw Wol looking wistfully out of the window and asked him, 'Would you like to sit outside?' He looked interested so I fixed him up with a perch just outside the French windows, where I could keep an eye on him from both the kitchen and the living room. He was very chuffed about this and spent his days sitting importantly on his perch, keeping a benevolent eye on the world about him. From time to time I popped out to exchange a few words with him and, depending on his mood at the time, he would favour me with a condescending nod or fix me with an inscrutable gaze before resuming his supervision of the outside world. The chickens and ducks ignored him, probably because they didn't know he was there; they rarely raised their eyes more than about three inches from the ground, experience having taught them that the chances of finding a worm or grain of corn in mid-air were pretty remote. Gussy spotted him immediately and came charging over demanding to know what Wol thought he was up to, setting himself up as clerk-of-works on his territory. Wol eyed him dispassionately for a moment or two then turned his back on him. I wouldn't have believed that so much contempt could be conveyed in such a small gesture. Gussy was completely nonplussed; shaking his head in bemusement he scuttled back to his swains grumbling and mumbling about stuck-up stuffed birds with delusions of grandeur. 'Just let him come down here,' he muttered, 'I'll show him!'

For about two weeks life went on without incident and then one morning I glanced out of the window to check on Wol – no Wol! I couldn't believe it; it couldn't have been more than three minutes since I'd last checked, and he'd been there then. I flew outside and started combing the grounds, the paddock, garden, donkey shelter, caravan, chicken houses, duck houses – nothing. After about an hour I was beginning to resign myself to the fact that I would never see Wol again when I caught a barely perceptible movement out of the corner of my eye – and there he was, sitting on the well and no more than about six feet from his perch. If he hadn't blinked I would never have spotted him – I had already passed the well about half a dozen times.

For the next three weeks the well remained Wol's chosen parking spot and then he went missing again. This time I ran him to earth on the strawberry barrel, again only yards from his previous resting place and again only after a frantic search. I fell on his neck, burbling with relief. 'Oh Wol, I thought I'd lost you!' He regarded me with wide-eyed wonder, 'What are you on about, I've been here all the time.' It suddenly occurred to me that this was all a game to him, a sort of owlish hide-and-seek. All right, you pop-eyed buffoon, I thought, if you want to play silly buggers then silly buggers it shall be. Two can play at that game. So when, two weeks later, he goes missing again I do not fly into a panic and go charging around the garden shrieking 'Wol, Wol, where are you, Wol?' like a raving lunatic. Oh no. This time I play it cool. I stroll aimlessly around the garden and paddock, stopping to inspect a flower here or a duck there. I have a word with a passing cat then wander over to exchange courtesies with the odd donkey. The one thing I am not doing is looking for a missing owl. Missing owl? What missing owl? So when

I hear the pitter-patter of little clawed feet behind me I look down with what I hope is well-simulated surprise. 'Why Wol, what are you doing here?' He regards me reproachfully. 'You didn't look for me. How can you find me if you don't look for me?' I feel mean and ashamed – I have spoiled his game.

I sat down on the garden bench and Wol hopped on to my lap. A wave of sheer contentment swept over me as I watched the donkeys cantering around playing tag in the paddock, the chickens proudly showing off their broods of powder puffs and the ducks dabbling happily in the pond. Only one thing marred this joyful scene; sitting on the chicken-house roof keeping an eye on the activity all around her looking for all the world like a chaperon at a deb's ball was Henrietta. This was her favourite time of year because she could indulge her passion for baby-watching. She was fascinated by the little ones and spent all her time either watching their antics from her viewing post or tagging along behind as they followed their mums around the garden. The chickens were so used to her by now that they simply took her presence as rearguard for granted. Possibly they figured that having an extra protector on hand was no bad thing. But it wrung my heart to see her always on the sidelines, never really a part of things. I was ashamed that, with all the traumas and catastrophes of the past year, the matter of getting her a companion had somehow been pushed into the background. Well, all that was over – as from now it had top priority.

Popping Wol back on his perch I went inside and rang Mr Newbury. A peacock? Of course – he had loads. When was I coming? Right now, I said. After checking that there was a free enclosure I brought Wol in, much to his disgust. It was still light, he chittered, he never came in as early as this, all the other animals

and birds were still out, it wasn't fair. 'I'll only be gone about an hour,' I told him, 'then you can go out again.' Unconvinced, he sat moodily on his perch, head huddled into his non-neck and sulked. Ah well, you can't please all of the creatures all of the time, I mused philosophically and not very originally.

When I got to Mr Newbury's, Jacey was sitting on the gatepost, waiting. By now he was beginning to know me and we enjoyed a fairly friendly relationship, or perhaps double-act would be a more accurate description, with me as the 'straight' man. He cocked a knowing eye at me. 'He's out' he intoned gleefully, 'he's not here!' 'Now don't start all that nonsense' I said, wondering why in heaven's name I was arguing with a jay, and particularly with one who always got the better of me, 'you know perfectly well he's not out.' 'Oh yes he is,' he insisted. 'He's not here. He's gone.' I saw Mr Newbury coming towards us and turned to Jacey. 'Not here, eh?' I enquired, 'Well, who's that then?' 'Oh, he is here,' he chirruped gaily, 'He is here. I'm a liar!' Yes, I thought, and a wicked little mischief-maker to boot!

Did I want a cock or a hen? Mr Newbury asked. Ah – very good question. I don't know. Feeling as stupid as I no doubt sounded I explained the position to Mr Newbury and sought his advice. 'Why not have a pair?' he suggested. 'Oh no,' I said, 'if I have a pair they'll stick together and Henrietta will be left out in the cold. That's not the idea at all.' He laughed. 'Peacocks usually have more than one mate. Henrietta and the other hen will be on equal footing.' I must have looked dubious because he added, 'Look, take a pair and if it doesn't seem to be working out the way you want I'll take one back and refund your money.' At the time this seemed extremely reasonable and I accepted gratefully.

136

It wasn't until I was halfway home that it struck me that I'd been conned again. I'd spent far more than I could afford buying two peafowl when I was hard-pressed to find the money for one, and although I appreciated his offer to take one back if there were problems, I think we both knew that once I got the birds home they were there for good. Well, just pray it works out, I told myself.

I hauled the sacks containing the peafowl out of the car, reflecting that there's nothing like starting the way you mean to go on; any inflated ideas they might have had about their station in life would undoubtedly have been dispelled by the indignity of travelling in a tatty old car, wrapped in sackcloth. 'The ashes come later,' I informed them. I had been a bit worried about the sacks but Mr Newbury assured me that this was the best way to transport peafowl without damaging their feathers. To my relief there were movements inside the sacks so at least they were still alive. Loading them on to my multipurpose trolley (an old pram, actually) I wheeled them over to the enclosure and off-loaded Solomon first. He was a Indian Blue, and a truly magnificent creature with brilliant plumage. His train hadn't grown yet but there were promising signs that it was on the way. Having installed him in the enclosure, much to his indignation, I untied Sheba's sack preparatory to decanting her. This was going to be a bit tricky; the problem was how to get her in without letting Solomon out. I decided to put her in complete with opened sack and leave it to her to find her own way out. That was the theory, anyway; what happened in practice was that she gave a convulsive jerk and was out of the sack and flying towards the woods before I had a chance to realise what was going on. Quickly shutting the door of the

137

enclosure to forestall any ideas Solomon might have had about joining Sheba, I set off after her.

Plodding across the paddock I couldn't help thinking what a good job it was that I wasn't a house-cleaning fanatic, because I'd never find time for housework anyway – all of my time seemed to be spent rounding up truant birds and animals. I walked through the woods, calling and calling her, all the time knowing that it was a lost cause. Having escaped from what to her must have been a frightening situation, it was hardly likely that Sheba would respond to the call of someone she didn't know and from whom she had fled in the first place. After about three hours I took a break to see to the other creatures and to apologise to an exceedingly disgruntled Wol for not keeping my promise to let him out again. He turned his back on me. I could see we had the makings of another Rufus here. Promising to make it up to him when things settled down a bit, I went to check on Solomon. He was pacing up and down his enclosure muttering crossly while Henrietta, perched on the top, tweeted soothingly to him. Well, that's promising, I thought.

Back to the woods to resume my search. I tried to find a spark of hope in the whole miserable business and, after scratching around in my mind, finally came up with one; being all-white, at least Sheba would be easy to spot. Yes, I told myself, and not only by you but by every gun-crazed lunatic, thick-headed vandal and peacock-napper in the area. When it began to get dark I abandoned my search and made my way back with a heavy heart.

About twenty yards from the edge of the woods, to my absolute delight I ran into Bertie who was apparently on his way to visit me. He whiffled at my hands and pockets but I had nothing for him. Usually when I go into the woods I fill my pockets with fruit or biscuits just in case I should run across Bertie or some other panhandler, but I had been in such a state that I'd completely forgotten. 'Come back with me,' I told him, 'and we'll see what we can find.' He frisked after me across the paddock and waited patiently at the kitchen door while I hastily mixed him a badger-type muesli. When he'd slurped it down he nuzzled my hand by way of thanks and joined me in a bit of slap and tickle, but after about ten minutes he was clearly anxious to be off. I dropped a kiss on his nose and watched as he ambled purposefully off towards the woods. I wonder if he's got a date, I mused. There was about him an air of jauntiness that suggested assignations and romantic dalliance. Well, bully for you, I thought.

Next morning I was up before dawn so that I could put in an hour or two searching for Sheba before starting the day proper. Stuffing my pockets full of corn and raisins I set off across the paddock to the accompaniment of excited braying from the donkeys and ear-splitting edritch calls from Solomon. How can such a beautiful creature make such a hideous din, I wondered. To my collection of home spun philosophical maxims I added a new one: 'People who keep peacocks shouldn't have neighbours.' Still, I thought hopefully, there's always a chance Sheba might hear him and come back. As I neared the edge of the woods I could just make out a white blob among the trees. 'It can't be,' I told myself not daring to hope. But as I got nearer I saw that it was indeed Sheba. Moving very slowly and quietly so as not to frighten her I edged as close as I dared and then very carefully put my hand in my pocket to take out some corn. The donkeys, who never miss a trick, recognised the gesture and, with a bellow of delight, came charging over. I watched helplessly as Sheba shot into the air and then vanished among the trees. Nice timing, donks, I muttered. I followed her into the woods and after about ten minutes spotted her in the undergrowth; unfortunately she spotted me too and in a flash she was gone. Clearly, this was never going to work. I left a trail of corn in the woods and alongside the paddock but, with silent apologies to Graham, on his side of the hedge. There was no point leaving the corn in the paddock as the chances were that the donkeys would eat it; and even if they didn't I thought it unlikely that Sheba would be prepared to run the gauntlet of five donkeys to get at it.

For the next three days I spent every spare, and quite a few not-so-spare moments searching for Sheba and leaving trails of corn all over the place; the wild birds must have thought it was Christmas. Every so often I caught a glimpse of her among the trees but could never get near enough to catch her. This might have gone on for ever if I hadn't run across Alf Turner one afternoon and, in response to his raised eyebrow, told him what I was up to. 'You'll never catch her like that,' he said. 'I'll show you how it's done.' Fishing about in his pockets he brought out a length of silky twine and I watched, fascinated, as he made a sort of noose and tied it with a slip knot. He spread it on the ground in a rough circle and, holding the free end, hid behind a tree. 'Put some corn inside the circle,' he whispered, 'then come and stand behind the tree and watch.' I did as he said and waited, hardly daring to breathe. Nothing happened for about half an hour and then I saw Sheba emerge from the shadows and start moving cautiously towards the corn. I held my breath as she approached the noose and then very warily stepped inside it. A second later it was all over – there was a squawk of surprise and a flapping of wings and before I had even realised what was

140

going on, Alf had removed the snare from her leg and was wrapping her in his coat. I wondered, fleetingly, what he normally used the snare for, but dismissed the thought as unworthy.

Alf carried Sheba back to the cottage and expertly decanted her into the enclosure, where she received an enthusiastic welcome from Solomon and Henrietta. Reflecting that it seemed a totally inadequate expression of my appreciation, I offered Alf a cup of tea and we settled down to half an hour of piggy prattle. 'I still think you're making a mistake,' he said, looking wistfully at the tangle of weeds that was rapidly taking over the garden. 'In a matter of weeks a little weaner would get rid of all that rubbish.' 'It's not rubbish,' I retorted indignantly, 'it's a Wild Garden. Since the farmers started grubbing out their hedges there's nowhere for the wild creatures to live and raise their families so they come here.' Even as I spoke, I wondered how truthful I was being. I loved the fact that the garden did attract wildlife, but was this the real or only reason I left it uncultivated? Or, perish the thought, was there an element of laissez faire involved? Bit of both probably, I decided.

After Alf left I went outside to see how things were going. Solomon and Sheba were pacing up and down in their enclosure, while Henrietta offered words of comfort in her gentle, tweeting voice. She was clearly much taken with the newcomers and spent all her time with them, leaving only to roost in the apple tree at night and joining them again the minute she got up in the morning. This might well work, I thought joyfully. After two weeks I decided they were ready to be released – if they weren't acclimatised by now the chances were they never would be. And they were obviously anxious to get out of the enclosure and enjoy some real freedom. Making my usual little speech about presenting them with the Freedom of the Establishment, trust they won't abuse the privilege, live in harmony with the other residents, no trespassing on neighbours' property, etc. I opened the door with a flourish and stood back to see what happened. At first, not a lot did. They just continued their pacing, stopping occasionally to stick their heads out of the doorway but making no attempt to come out. At last Henrietta, who had also been anxiously awaiting developments, hopped down from her vantage point and daintily stepped into the enclosure with them. In her best hostess manner she indicated the open door and graciously invited them to take a turn around the garden with her. They watched as she tripped elegantly out again and stood just outside, waiting for them to follow. Solomon and Sheba consulted for a moment or two then, with a word to Sheba which I interpreted as 'I'll go first – there might be tigers', Solomon squared his shoulders and marched manfully out through the doorway. After a few moments' indecision Sheba joined him. Then the three of them set off on a tour of inspection, with Henrietta happily acting as guide and filler-in of background information. I kept an eye on them for the rest of the day and was overjoyed to see that the three of them really were a unit, with Henrietta an integral part of it. She was plainly delighted with her new companions and I reproached myself bitterly for having left it so long. The fact that Percy, her previous 'companion' had been such a disaster was really no excuse for not having provided her with another one sooner.

I waited anxiously to see what would happen about sleeping arrangements. When darkness began to fall, Henrietta led Solomon and Sheba over to the apple tree

and, with instructions to watch carefully, went through her nightly ritual of circling the tree, calculating the distance, mentally selecting and then discarding several possible alternatives and carrying out a few dummy runs before taking off and landing on one of the lower branches; a few minutes pause to get her breath back before she scrambled up to her accustomed branch, from where she peered down anxiously at Solomon and Sheba, entreating them to join her. Solomon looked at Sheba and Sheba looked at Solomon, then they both looked at Henrietta. Agreement reached, they flapped their wings and took off. Seconds later all three of them were comfortably settled in a neat row on the branch. My delight that Henrietta not only had friends to spend her days with but also sleeping companions to keep her warm at night was sharpened by another, less worthy consideration. I would be spared the thankless chore of rounding up the peafowl and herding them into the enclosure every night.

Under Henrietta's guidance, Solomon and Sheba quickly settled into the routine of life here; never having queened it in the landscaped grounds of a stately home like most of their genre they accepted their undistinguished surroundings without question. An

143

added bonus was the unmistakable, and wholly bogus, touch of class they gave to the place. Even the thistles and nettles took on an air of exoticism when they were around. By contrast, the other birds looked undeniably drab and I found myself worrying about them developing an inferiority complex and sinking into a decline. What were the symptoms of neurosis in birds, I wondered? Would they retire into themselves, leading solitary lives and speaking only when spoken to? Or would they escape into a fantasy world, totally removed from the nitty-gritty of everyday life? Or over-compensate by becoming loud-mouthed, ill-tempered bullies, throwing their weight about . . . I pulled myself up short – there was something horribly familiar about the image this conjured up. God help us, I thought – not a horde of Gussie-clones!

CHAPTER 13

It was a wonderful summer and I spent practically every daylight hour outside. Not only because I think it's a criminal waste to be indoors when the sun is shining (if the Good Lord intended us to stay indoors he would send rain and blizzards), but also because I wanted to be with the animals, and particularly with Wol. Being a very sociable creature, he was tickled to death about this. 'Aren't you lucky,' burbled my London friends, displaying their Mediterranean tans, 'just sitting outside all day lapping up the sun!' *Sitting* outside? You must be joking! For one thing, there's always so much to do around the place that there's never time for such luxuries. For another, the sinfulness of lounging around doing nothing on a working day has been so deeply impressed upon me from childhood that even now I can't sit down during daylight hours without expecting to be struck by lightning. And in any case, there could be absolutely no question of relaxing while Wol was around. The way he saw it, if I was outside it could be for only one reason – to provide entertainment and diversion for him. He wasn't so far wrong, at that.

He was always deeply interested in whatever I was

doing, watching intently until he got the hang of it then, unable to contain his impatience a moment longer, swooping down to tell me that I was doing it all wrong, *this* was how it should be done. Particularly if I was potting up plants; this was the activity he most enjoyed being involved in (I think he called it 'helping').

Picking his way delicately from pot to pot, shredding a leaf here, squashing a stem there, occasionally stopping to pull a plant out by its roots, study it carefully for a moment or two and then toss it away, until he reached the pot I was working on. Eyes wide with excitement, he would perch on the edge of the pot and scrabble away industriously at the compost until the consistency was to his liking. Then, with a blissful sigh, he eased himself gently into the pot and took a dustbath. Conscience-striken that I had neglected to provide this essential facility, I immediately set to work constructing a dustbath of Palladian splendour, with every grain of dust carefully selected and sifted to provide the ultimate in comfort and luxury. 'There, Wol,' I said proudly when I'd finished, I'll bet there isn't an owl in the world with such a super dustbath.' He gave it a cursory glance and, clearly underwhelmed, went back to his flowerpot. 'Nothing personal,' he assured me, 'It's just that this is more fun.'

Birds of prey rarely drink but they do like to splash about in water. I can always tell when it's bath-time for Sid the kestrel because he starts shrieking his head off. Prey birds feel particularly vulnerable when they're bathing, so I assume that Sid's screeching is meant as a warning to predators to keep away. My own feeling is that if he'd just shut up and get on with it, instead of announcing his intentions to the entire world, he'd probably be a whole lot safer. Liz, his mate, hasn't uttered so much as a peep in all the years she's been

146

here, so when she takes a bath Sid obligingly does her screeching for her.

I bought Wol a paddling pool (a cat litter tray, actually) and he watched, agog, as I set it down on the patio and filled it with water. After much vigorous head-nodding he fluttered down from his perch and waddled over to it. Standing on tiptoe he peered over the edge and – good gracious! Another owl in there! He stepped back to consider the situation, gave a couple of ponderous nods then very cautiously stretched his head forward and took another furtive peep. It was still there! Gingerly he picked his way around the edge of the tray, never taking his eyes from the water. It was following him! This was too much! Every feather a quiver with indignation he hopped onto the edge of the tray and plunged in. Owls are supposed to be inscrutable, but Wol's face is an open book, registering curiosity, alarm, affront, pleasure or whatever other emotion he happens to be feeling. I watched with delight as his initial surprise at the shock of the water turned to interest and then, as the potential of this lovely wet stuff dawned on him, to utter joy. Bobbing his head and flapping his wings he applied himself enthusiastically to the task of seeing how much water he could displace in the least possible time. Dripping from head to toe, I remarked sourly that, gratified as I was with his obvious appreciation of his paddling pool, a little restraint would not come amiss. He assumed his martyred expression – but I wanted to share this lovely experience with you!

From then on he was in and out of his bath all day long. He emerged from his ablutions looking absolutely deplorable – a bedraggled, waterlogged bunch of drooping feathers. A brisk shake then a lopsided waddle over to the step where, wings outstretched, he

147

sprawled out to dry, exuding utter bliss from every feather.

It wasn't long before the ducks and geese, alerted by the sounds of splashing, trundled over to investigate. Although they have a large pond of their own, any new source of water is an irresistible attraction for them. Leave the kitchen door open for more than a minute and the chances are that one of these opportunists, with more hope than wit, will try to squeeze itself into the cat's drinking bowl. Wol had finished his dip and was drying out. I was keeping an eye on him, because he is particularly vulnerable when he's wet, when the first assault took place. A procession of ducks and geese, led of course by Gussie, marched in single file up to the Wol-sized tray and, with much shoving and jockeying for position, tried to squeeze into it. Wol, spread-eagled on the step, stiffened with outrage at this gross violation of his territory. Chittering with rage he drew himself up and charged over to do battle with the invaders. I had to admire his guts – a tatty little handful of dripping feathers ready to take on a raiding party of twenty or more assorted ducks and geese, but I couldn't stand by and allow him to commit hari-kari in defence of his pond. Before I had a chance to grab him he was in among them, hurling abuse and threatening mayhem if they didn't get off his property THIS MINUTE. To my astonishement the invaders immediately deflated and, looking sheepish and embarrassed, all turned tail and shuffled off – even Gussie. From then on Wol guarded his pond jealously – he only had to catch sight of a duck within twenty yards of his territory and the battle was on.

So I was very surprised, a few days later, to find Wol happily sharing his pond with Olga. Surprised and pleased, because Olga is a particular favourite of mind.

She and Oscar, her mate, are the only Muscovies I have, the other ducks apart from Quaggy being a motley assortment of unidentifiable origin. Muscovies are odd sort of creatures; they are much larger than the average duck and, though it grieves me to say it, really rather grotesque. They don't quack – Olga cheeps and Oscar does a nice line in heavy breathing. In fact, some experts say that they are not really ducks at all, but geese. Certainly Olga has no doubt that she is not a duck and refuses to have anything to do with the other ducks. At the same time, she seems to have no affinity with the geese either. As Oscar suffers no such identity crisis, happily mating with anything that comes his way – duck, chicken, cockerel, Muscovy, even on one occasion trying it on with Gussie, who very smartly put him in his place – Olga's is a somewhat lonely life.

I think this bothers me more than it does her; so far as she is concerned, she was put into this world for one reason only – to brood and raise as many mini-Muscovies as time permitted.

Each year she lays her quota of thirteen eggs, sits on them for what seems like several months and eventually emerges triumphantly with thirteen little pom-poms. But this year something had gone tragically wrong. Of her first clutch, only one had hatched and this was a very sickly baby that died within a few days. After a decent period of mourning, in which I joined, she set to and laid another clutch. Again only one hatched and again tragedy struck. A few days later her baby drowned in the donkey bucket. Olga was inconsolable; she moped around all day, refusing to eat or take any interest in life. Dispiritedly she collected stones or bits of donkey dung which she took back to her nest and sat on, but her heart wasn't really in it. So I was overjoyed when she struck up a friendship with Wol – two of my favourite creatures getting together! No match-making mama could have been more delighted. Not that there were any romantic overtones in their relationship. So far as Olga was concerned Wol filled the gap left by the babies she had lost; all she wanted was to love and mother him. As for Wol, always the opportunist, he knew when he was on to a good thing – a human mum to feed him and provide entertainment at night, and a feathered mum to protect him during the day. What more could any Wol want

Every morning, as soon as I let the ducks out Olga would waddle over to Wol's perch and cheep anxiously to him. Whereupon Wol would hop down, chittering like mad, to assure her that he was all right, honest he was. This was not good enough for Olga – she had to be sure. Every square inch of Wol had to be minutely

150

examined before she was satisfied that nothing untoward had happened to her foster-baby overnight. Wol took her ministrations in good part, probably deciding that discretion was the better part of valour, Olga being at least three times as big as him. Inspection completed, Wol hopped back on to his perch while Olga settled down on the ground just below him and assumed her self-appointed role of Wol Watcher and Guardian-in-Chief. She took her duties very seriously, staying at her post all day except for the occasional meal break. I really think, if it hadn't been for Wol, she would never have got over the depression. But soon she started to lay again and each day I counted the eggs . . . 10, 11, 12, 13. When the last egg had been laid, she abandoned her post to brood them. Poor Wol was desolate; he couldn't understand why his good friend had forsaken him. Every morning when he heard the ducks' excited quacking after being released he hopped down from his perch and waited expectantly for Olga to come and give him her daily inspection. I ached for him as I watched his eager anticipation slowly turn to disappointment. His solemn little face wrinkled with disappointment and hurt, he turned beseeching, saucer-wide eyes to me – 'Was it something I said?' I assured him that he was in no way to blame for Olga's defection and, when his gaze turned from sorrowful to reproachful, that neither was I!

Thinking that a little diversion might take Wol's mind off Olga I took him for walks around the garden and paddock every day; who knows, I thought, he might strike up a friendship with one of the other birds. He didn't, of course, but after a few days he started to perk up again and take a bit of interest in what was going on around him. It was during one of these therapeutic walks that Ned Malloy came into my life.

We had completed our tour of the garden and were just about to go into the paddock when it struck me that something was wrong; the donkeys hadn't set up the usual ear-splitting cacophony that the sight of me doing anything not directly connected with their personal well-being usually triggers off. 'They've gone,' I thought. 'They're trampling through Graham's wheat or eating Julia's hay or chasing Alec's chickens up a tree.' It had been some time since they'd last broken out and I suppose I was getting a bit complacent. And then I saw them, standing in a semi-circle in the middle of the paddock totally absorbed in what I took to be a sack of potatoes but which on closer inspection turned out to be a gnome-sized man wrapped in several layers of rags, each layer tattier than the one beneath. It was a boiling hot day and the aroma of steaming flesh he exuded was as heady as champagne, albeit a little less appetising.

He didn't look up as I approached, and neither did the donkeys who were gazing at him with the kind of soulful adoration that I'm lucky to get even when I'm feeding them specially selected, highly expensive donkey delights. He was talking to them and, intrigued, I eaves-dropped shamelessly: '. . . and the hills are as green as the emeralds that men give their lives to dig out of the earth. And running through them with a babble like a maiden's laugh are the little streams, so clear you can see the fishes playing in the rocks below. There are gentle mists and breezes as sweet as a baby's breath. And the animals running free and wild and happy as the day is long. Are there donkeys there, do I hear you asking? To be sure, and isn't it the place where good donkeys go when they die?' It is many, many years since I was last in Ireland, but listening to him describing his homeland in that soft lilting voice brought the image of it back so sharply that I could almost smell the peat burning. He caught sight of me and without a break in flow and with no sign of embarrassment, as though it were the most natural thing in the world to be sitting in somebody else's field delivering a travelogue to five enraptured donkeys, he observed, 'Ah, 'tis the good lady herself, and how do you find yourself today?' I told him that I found myself very nicely, thank you, and would he like a beer? I thought I might pick up a few tips from him on the art of hypnotising donkeys – never know when it might come in handy! He accepted graciously and we sat down on the garden seat.

Studying him covertly I decided that he must be least 150 years old. His face was the colour and texture of a pickled walnut, deeply etched with dirt-ingrained lines, and his pale blue eyes seemed to be swimming in pools of gelatine. Still in that soft, beguiling voice he told me that his name was Ned Malloy and that he was born in County Wicklow but his people were tinkers and they travelled all over. He had come to England in his twenties and one by one his brothers had followed him, thinking that the living would be easier here. He was a horse dealer and that brought him to the reason for his visit; two of his ponies, Molly and Bridie, had broken out of their field and he thought they might have come here. I pointed out to him that as my menage was noted for the frequency with which the resident equines left it, it seemed unlikely that his fugitives would choose it as a place to lie up. Not at all, not at all, he assured me, the thing with horses and especially donkeys, was that wherever they were they wanted to be somewhere else. A bit like some people, he added dolefully, thinking no doubt of his beloved Ireland. He gave me detailed descriptions of his missing ponies so that I'd recognise them, although the number of peopleless ponies passing this way is so minimal that if two did turn up I think I would probably have assumed that they were his anyway. But I promised to be on the look-out. 'Tell them Ned says they're to come home at once or they'll get no oats,' he instructed me as he left. From time to time I looked out for them but it wasn't until later afternoon that I saw the ponies in the next field, chatting to the donkeys over the fence. Feeling no end of a fool I went over to them and said firmly, 'Ned says you're to go home at once or you'll get no oats.' To my astonishment, not to mention that of the donkeys, they immediately turned tail and headed off for home. The donkeys, awestruck, turned to one another: 'Did you see that?' Then, to me: 'My goodness, aren't you clever?' And I thought I saw a gleam of admiration in their eyes. 'I'd be a darned sight cleverer if I could do it with you,' I retorted. They looked shocked. 'We're *donkeys*! We're supposed to be bloody-minded.'

The next day Ned was back, shyly clutching a bunch of wild flowers picked from the woods, 'just to be saying thank you for sending those young rascals home,' he explained. Intrigued, I asked him how he knew it was me. He looked surprised. 'Weren't they after telling me?' he replied. I thanked heaven that my language towards his truants had been above reproach – the last thing I wanted was a couple of ponies wandering around the neighbourhood telling everybody that I cussed like a fishwife! Ned looked hot and tired so I gave him a drink and settled down to enjoy a further instalment of his life story. He had come to live in the area about twelve years ago; a friendly farmer let him use one of his fields to keep his horses in, in return for doing odd jobs around the place, and he had put up a hut in the field to provide living accommodation for himself. He had never married, never having felt the need. 'Why would I be wasting my youth on a woman? But now, in his declining years, 'It mightn't be such a bad idea to have someone to look after me.' Chauvinist pig, I thought.

He was back again the next day, this time bearing gifts in the form of not-quite-ripe blackberries. And the next day, and the day after that. It wasn't until the conversation turned to his taste in women – 'I've always had an eye for a woman that looks like a woman' – this was an appreciative leer at my generous proportions, that it dawned on me that he was chatting me up! It was so long since I'd been chatted-up that I'd completely failed to recognise the signs! It was all beginning to fall into place – his interest in the cottage coupled with his complaints about his draughty hut; his hints about needing somebody to look after him in his dotage; the gifts of unripe blackberries and wilting dandelions. Crafty old bugger, I fumed

Over the next two weeks he became bolder in his approach, paying me outrageous compliments (in fairness, I have to admit that he was even more flattering about the cottage than he was about me!) and I found that I had no weapons against him. It's impossible to pour cold water on someone who's so besotted with his own eloquence that he doesn't even hear what you're saying. And even though I was now very cagey indeed, the proposal when it came still caught me completely unawares. He was talking about his faith and his church when suddenly he said, 'Won't it be splendid now, the two of us kneeling at the altar exchanging vows?' It took a good two minutes for me to recover my breath and my equilibrium sufficiently to answer him, and even then the best I could manage was, 'Is this a proposal?' He grasped my hand and said, 'Isn't , that what I've been telling you all this time? We'll be married and live

155

happily together, just the two of us in your cosy little cottage.' It occurred to me that he wasn't proposing to me, he was proposing to the cottage – I was just the go-between. I searched for an answer that would be absolutely, unmistakably final without being too much of a snub. And then it came to me; I said, quite truthfully, touched as I was by his offer, marriage between us was out of the question because he was Catholic and I was Jewish. He was silent for a while and I really thought I'd cracked it. Then his face brightened and he said, 'Ah, to be sure now, Catholic or Jew, what does it matter so long as we're all Christians?'

He was back the next day, ardour undampened and resolution strengthened and I felt the beginnings of panic swelling up inside. My fear was that he'd wear me down by sheer persistence. It's one thing to take in homeless birds and animals but if I started extending the facility to people there was no knowing where it might end. No, it had to be stopped here and now. I was sorry, in a way because when Ned could be kept off the subject of well-stacked wives-of-convenience he was quite an interesting conversationalist. But the price was too high.

The next time he called I didn't offer him a drink and I didn't stop to chat. Explaining that I had a million things to do I just went on with my chores. 'I'll help you,' said he, trotting along behind me like a well-trained terrier on the scent of a rat. I felt a wave of hysteria rising and was terrified that it would get out of hand and I'd end up doing him a serious mischief. 'Look,' I said firmly, 'I'm always pleased to see you for a chat but you must get one thing quite clear. Marriage is out of the question because I'm already married. I don't talk about it because he's in prison, doing a stretch for Grievous Bodily Harm.' Seeing a spark of alarm in Ned's eyes, I warmed to my theme. 'He's usually fairly harmless, considering he weighs seventeen stone, but he's very jealous. He caught this bloke looking at me in a pub and he broke his back. He got five years for that, but he'll be out in three weeks.' For the first time during our relationship he was silent, although I could see by the twitching of his lips that something was struggling to get out. After what seemed like an eternity he said in a strangled whisper, 'I'll be going now,' and with a terrified glance around him he tottered off. And that was the end of my brief romance.

CHAPTER 14

Townspeople are always saying to me 'But don't you find it dreadfully dull, living in the country? Nothing ever happens.' I stare at them, open-mouthed. Hardly a day passes that something doesn't happen; true, they are rarely events of earth-shattering proportions but the spice they add to life is incalculable. It's impossible to describe the joy of waking up each morning, not knowing what the day ahead holds. When I lived in London I knew exactly what each day would bring forth and any surprises usually turned out to be unpleasant ones. Getting bogged down in a traffic jam – nothing novel about that. Car breaking down – so what else is new? Of course I've had my share of not-so-pleasant surprises here, but if nothing else at least they've been different.

One of the happier surprises was when Quaggy brought home a bride. I don't know where he found her, and far-ranging enquiries brought no clue as to her origins. If she had been a mallard I could have understood it; wild ducks frequently fly over here and it was not beyond the realms of possibility that an unattached female had spotted Quaggy and been instantly smitten. But this was a domestic duck, a Khaki Campbell. They were clearly very taken with each other and I was delighted for Quaggy; quite apart from anything else, she was Quaggy-sized and a far more suitable mate for him than a goose, not to mention a human being! I named her Margie and informed her that she was very welcome to regard this as her home – any friend of Quaggy's was a friend of mine. She showed her appreciation by laying a large, richly-yolked egg every day.

Inbetween times I was keeping a watchful eye on Olga as her eggs were due to hatch any time now. When I spotted a downy little head peering out from under her wing one morning I was overjoyed. Sadly this was the only duckling to hatch and after another three days Olga abandoned the rest of the clutch and introduced her baby to the outside world. Wol spotted her immediately and, delighted to see his old friend again, gave a squawk of delight and hippety-hopped over to welcome her. Understandably, after all she had been through to produce this one duckling, Olga wasn't taking any chances; she flew at Wol, screaming imprecations. He was totally unprepared for this and came scuttling back to hide behind my legs, whimpering softly. He was terribly hurt; Olga was his friend and he only wanted to tell how much he'd missed her and take a look at her baby. He wouldn't have hurt it. I tried to comfort him but he was inconsolable. He never entirely forgave Olga and although they resumed their friendship later, things were never quite the same between them.

Later that day I went out to remove the rest of Olga's eggs and Wol came with me. I was picking each egg up and examining it to see if I could find a clue to its failure when suddenly Wol started chittering excitedly. I

159

looked up and saw that he was rolling one of the eggs around with his beak. I took it from and, to my amazement, heard faint squeaks from it. Closer inspection showed that the shell was beginning to break – this little chap was about ready to enter the world of the living. Stopping only to pat Wol on the head and tell him what a clever little owl he was, I dashed into the kitchen and dunked the egg in a bowl of warm water to soften the shell. In the ordinary way it would have got all the moisture it needed from its potential mum but this one was strictly on its own. After a good soak I tucked it into my bra and awaited developments. It was now tweeting lustily but I felt a bit daft going around with a chirping bosom. Wol was fascinated – he kept climbing on to my lap or shoulder, depending on whether I was sitting or standing, so that he could put his downy little head to my chest and tune in to the cheeping. A look of wonder spread over his face: I didn't know people could tweet – I thought it was only birds!

Breaking out of the shell was obviously pretty hard work because by bedtime my foundling was still only half out. I didn't get a lot of sleep that night, what with the tweeting and having to lie on my back in case I squashed the emergent duckling. By morning he was out and my body looked like a mosaic, with bits of eggshell sticking to virtually every part of my anatomy.  I looked at my hatchling with some misgiving – he really was pathetic. All skin and bone, bedraggled fluff clinging wetly to his body, head drooping. I dried him off gently with my hair-dryer and very soon my ugly duckling began to turn into, if not a swan, certainly a very pretty little chap. His downy feathers fluffed out and as he became stronger he was able to hold his head up – he really looked quite perky. He was pale yellow with brown markings on his wings – a typical Muscovy duckling. Olga would be pleased!

After dark I went out to feed Olga and while she had her head stuck in the dish I very gently slipped the little duckling under her. Quick as a flash she shoved him out again. I tried again, with the same result. I could see that this wasn't going to work. After shutting Olga up for the night, I took my orphan back into the cottage. Well, Boris, I said, meet your new mum. Boris cheeped happily – as far as he was concerned, I *was* his mum. After all, I had hatched him and mine was the first face he's seen on entering the world , so it was a natural enough assumption. My main concern was how Wol would react to having this fluffy interloper about the place. Would he resent the presence of another bird? Even worse, would he regard little Boris as a potential meal-on-the-hoof? As it turned out, I needn't have worried. Having been instrumental in rescuing Boris from an eggy grave, Wol took a proprietoral interest in him, protecting him from over-curious cats and, as he became stronger and more adventurous, discouraging him from potentially suicidal activities.

When Boris was about ten days old I decided he was ready to sample the delights of the world outside. We set off in procession around the garden, Boris following me and twittering with excitement at this great adventure, and Wol closely following Boris, chittering anxiously at every danger, real or imagined, to his foster-baby's safety. When Boris encountered his first puddle he was ecstatic – he plunged straight in, bobbing and diving and splashing joyously. Wol, horrified at this foolhardiness, plunged into the puddle (it was only about half an inch deep anyway) and very gently nudged Boris out, much to his indignation.

While we were out we came upon Olga, also taking

161

her baby out for an airing. We exchanged courtesies and went our respective ways. She showed absolutely no interest in Boris, nor he in her. A few yards farther on Boris stopped at another puddle while I kept going. Suddenly realising that I was not within the regulation six inches Boris gave out with his 'Mum-where-are-you-wait-for-me' squawk. Olga stopped in her tracks – she might not have recognised Boris but she certainly recognised the call. She marched purposefully over to Boris and said, 'I would guess something along the lines of 'FOLLOW ME'. Boris regarded this large and rather unprepossessing stranger with horror and fled screaming with terror to hide behind my legs, closely followed by the ever-protective Wol. Olga and I confronted each other. Her eyes were blazing and she was the very picture of outraged motherhood. I had her baby and she wanted him back – NOW! For my part, I was all for returning Boris to his natural mum; not only did she know far more about raising and rearing baby ducks than I would ever know, she also had another little duckling for Boris to play with. Wol was a marvellous guardian but, from Boris' point of view, he wasn't much of a playmate. Boris would be much better off with his own family; the only problem was getting Boris to see it this way. I decided to try the tuck-him-under-her-while-she's not-looking ploy again, convinced that Olga wouldn't reject him now. Which she didn't – this time it was Boris who did the rejecting. Five times I tucked him under her and five times he came scuttling out, crying plaintively and making me feel like the kind of mum who abandons her offspring in a telephone box.

I took Boris out every day and I was finding it increasingly embarrassing because Olga followed us everywhere, vainly trying to lure Boris away. Every-

where we went I could feel her accusing eyes following me. Ducknapper, they said. Child stealer. Nest-robber. I felt awful. Then one day, while Olga and I were engaged in our fruitless dialogue – she accusing me of alienation of her baby's affections and me trying to explain that the last thing I wanted was to keep her and Boris apart – I noticed another little drama being played out in the background. Clearly fed up with the grown-ups' eternal bickering, the two little ducklings had turned to each other for diversion and were snuggled up together at our feet. This might well be the answer, I thought, and crept quietly away. I hadn't covered more than about six feet before Boris came scuttling after me closely followed, to my horror, by Olga's baby. Oh my God, I thought, that's really done it! But Olga had the situation well in hand. Just one

163

'Come-back-here-At-ONCE' peep and her baby was back at her side. But not Boris, alas. In the end it was the little ones who resolved the problem. As they got more and more attached to one another Boris became increasingly reluctant to leave his playmate. Then one night, when Olga and her baby went into their enclosure, Boris – with an apologetic glance at me – followed them in and setled down to sleep with them, and I knew he had made his choice. I tried not to catch Olga's eye because the triumph and smugness she was exuding were well-nigh insufferable. I was truly pleased, both for her and the ducklings, but I couldn't help thinking that she might have been a little more restrained in her victory.

Wol took Boris' defection philosophically. Deep down I think he wasn't all that sorry. As Boris grew bigger and more wilful, Wol had been finding it increasingly difficult to keep him under control. Also, I think he was pleased to be Number One bird-around-the-house again!

CHAPTER 15

Winter came and again we were all confined to quarters. I think Wol felt it more than any of us; he missed his daily sessions in the garden desperately and it broke my heart to see him sitting on the windowsill, nose pressed wistfully to the window and looking for all the world like a feathered Bisto Kid. And then I had an idea. As soon as the path was clear and I was able to get the car out again, I said to him 'How would you like a trip out to blow away the cobwebs?' His face brightened and he nodded enthusiastically. I took him out to the car and he hopped onto the steering wheel; turning his little mophead in an almost complete circle he looked all around him and informed the other furred and feathered residents squawkily: 'Look at me – I'm driving!' 'Oh no you're not,' I corrected him. 'Any driving that's going to be done will be done by me.' He accepted this philosophically and settled himself cosily on my head. After the first excursion I had only to say, 'Come on, Wol, let's go for a drive,' and he would waddle over to the car and wait while I opened the door, feathers quivering with excitement at this Great Adventure. My greatest worry was how he would react to the inevitable attention he would attract from people unaccustomed

165

to seeing a tawny owl taking the air in broad daylight, but he took it entirely in his stride, regarding the homage paid to him as no less than his due. In fact, he was a lot more patient with people than I was; I got so tired of answer questions about him that after a while my responses became almost automatic:

Question: How did you train him to sit on your head?
Answer: You don't train an owl. If he wants to sit on your head, he sits on your head.
Q: Does he talk?
A: He's an owl, not a parrot (If I'm feeling particularly tetchy the answer is: 'Only to people he knows, never to strangers'.)
Q: Isn't he messy?
A: Yes, very. (In fact, being a meat-eater he is a lot more messy than our average domesticated bird. Fortunately the decor of my cottage is Lived-In rather than Homes & Gardens and strategically placed newspapers help reduce the damage.)
Q: How did you get him so tame?
A: I didn't. Owls are like people – some are friendly, some aren't. Wol just happens to be a particularly matey bird.

The question that really sends the blood rushing to my head is: How much do you want for him?' After a while I started saying, absolute po-faced, '£350'. That soon shuts them up – or most of them. I still remember with horror the wealthy Arab who, without so much as a raised eyebrow, drew out his wallet and started counting out £20 notes. 'Stop! Stop!' I shrieked, 'It was only a joke! There isn't enough money in the world to induce me to part with Wol.' I thought about this later when someone asked me what I would do if I was offered £1,000 for Wol. I had to answer honestly that I couldn't think of anything I could buy for a thousand pounds that would give me half the pleasure I get from Wol.

But as winter drew to a close and I watched Wol's obvious longing to be outside I couldn't suppress a niggle of worry about the unnaturalness of his life. He should be outside with other birds for company, I thought, not spending all his time with cats and people. What he needs, I decided, is a companion of his own kind – another owl, in fact. So when, a month or two later, Jim rang to ask if I could take in a baby owl, I was convinced that this was fate. He told me that the fledgling had fallen out of its nest but was unharmed; it just needed care and protection until it was big enough to fend for itself. It occurred to me that no other baby birds seem to fall out of their nests to the extent that owls do and I couldn't help wondering, particularly when Wol was being especially trying, whether they really do fall out or whether their mums – patience tried to the limit – shove them out! Anyway, I was thrilled to bits about it and couldn't wait to share the good news with Wol. 'Oh Wol,' I babbled excitedly, 'you're going to have a companion – another little one to keep you company! Just think of it! He thought about it for a moment or two, decided that it was no big deal, and went back to his contemplation of the world outside.

Toby duly arrived, a pathetic little bundle of fluff about the same size as Wol had been when he first came. But there the resemblance ended, and if I had needed confirmation of the fact that Wol was a one-off, this was it. Toby cowered in his box, convulsed with fear and crying tremulously, and any ideas I might have had

167

about introducing him to Wol were immediately dispelled. At the moment Toby was in no condition to meet anybody, and certainly not such an over-the-top extrovert as Wol. I installed Toby in a comfortable box on top of the heated Hostess tray in the study and left him alone to get over his shock. By next morning he had stopped crying but was still very frightened. I left him some minced beef laced with chopped feathers but when I went up to see him later he hadn't touched it. I took it away and replaced it with minced chicken but he didn't eat that either. I was reluctant to hand-feed him because he would be released eventually and I didn't want him to become too attached to me. Not that there was much likelihood of that, the way things were at the moment. But in any case the first priority was to get some food inside him otherwise the question of his release would become purely academic.

I sat Toby on my lap and, prising his beak open, gently pushed bits of food down his throat with special tweezers. He didn't put up any resistance but he made it quite clear that if I expected any co-operation I could think again. He kept his beak clamped tightly shut between mouthfuls, so that I had to prise it open again before putting in the next one. As each feeding session took over half an hour and he had to be fed every two hours, it didn't leave much time for anything else. This went on for about a week and then, to my joy, he started opening his beak without any help from me. Soon after he began taking the food from my fingers and within another few days he was feeding himself. He was beginning to look quite perky and it wasn't long before he abandoned his box and started exploring the study. But he was still very nervous of me, clicking like a locust every time I went near him, which augured well for his life in the wild.

I fixed him up with a perch by the window which he used as a stepping stone to the top of the bookshelf. After cogitating for a moment or two, he started tugging at one of the books with his beak until it fell to the floor; he inspected the gap and then pulled out another book and then a third. Excavation completed to his satisfaction, he squeezed into the space left and settled himself comfortably into what he was convinced was Invisibility. All it needs is Wol at the other end and I'd have a pair of book-ends, I mused. If there's one thing I've learned about birds and beasts it's that the more trouble you take to fix them up with a warm, soft, comfortable home, the more likely they are to reject it in favour of something hard, knobbly and totally uninviting.

The study is next door to my bedroom and at night I could hear Toby industriously going about whatever business that young owls go about at night. His feathers were coming along nicely and he was growing fast; I judged that he was about ready to meet Wol. After much consideration I decided to bring Wol to Toby, rather than the other way about. Wol might resent an intruder on his patch and duff Toby up, thereby nipping in the bud what might otherwise have been a promising relationship. Also Toby would feel more confident in familiar surroundings whereas Wol's sense of security was so well established that it wouldn't matter to him if the meeting took place down a mine-shaft. Most important of all, there would be no cats around upstairs to worry Toby. I opened the door leading to the stairs and said 'Come on, Wol.' He looked a bit mystified – he knew it wasn't bedtime yet because the telly was still on, and in any case he had been sleeping in the sitting-room since Toby's arrival. Still, always game for a bit of a lark, he waddled over and started his old routine of one step up, three steps back.

We eventually got to the top and he waited by the study door until I opened it. With a hoot of delight he made straight for the window and immediately went into his Tarzan act, swinging from the Venetian blind. He hadn't noticed Toby yet, but Toby had noticed him all right and was watching him with a mixture of interest and apprehension. So was I, for that matter. Suddenly, in mid-swing, Wol caught sight of Toby and was so taken aback that he lost his hold on the cord and promptly dropped to the floor. Not in the least deterred, he picked himself up, marched resolutely over to the bookcase and started climbing it. Both Toby and I held our breath, wondering what was coming next. We soon found out. Wol heaved himself onto the top of the book shelf, picked his way daintily across the books to where Toby was huddled in the not-so-hidey-hole, and shoved him off. Toby was taken completely by surprise – whatever he had expected, it certainly wasn't this. He sat where he had fallen, looking deeply hurt and chittering plaintively. Wol peered at him over the top of the bookshelf and told him to get lost. Shocked at this appalling behaviour, I grabbed Wol and took him downstairs, much to his indignation. He was only having a bit of fun, he complained, and I had spoilt it. I always spoilt everything, it wasn't fair. He hated me and as soon as he could fly he was going to leave home, so there! 'Have you done?' I asked him. 'Is that it, or is there more?' He considered this for a moment or two: Yes, that was it. 'Good,' I said. If there is one single thing about animals that sets them above people it is, for me anyway, the fact that they don't bear a grudge. They may sulk or swear if they're upset, but once it's over it's over. No recriminations, no acts of revenge, nothing. Of course it might well be because their memories are poor and they simply don't remember what it was that upset them, but I prefer to think that they've just got nice forgiving natures.

Well, one thing was for sure – the time was not yet ripe for a Toby–Wol alliance. We were well into spring now and Wol was already spending most of the day outside. I decided to put Toby into an outside enclosure so that he and Wol would get used to seeing one another about the place. Also, it would give Toby a chance to get used to the outdoor life and, most important of all for his future survival, he would have less contact with me. I put a large barrel with a hole in the side into his enclosure so that he'd have somewhere to get away from it all during the day, and installed him on a leafy branch. All the enclosures are built around trees so that the inmates have plenty of cover and a wide variety of branches for roosting, sleeping or just meditating. Toby seemed happy enough in his new home, but it was difficult to tell; there was something about the configuration of his face that made him look exactly like a mournful monkey and his permanent expression was one of deep misery. But watching him hopping about from branch to branch, or just sitting sedately on top of his barrel watching the world go by, I was pretty sure that he was as content as any wild bird can be in captivity. 'Have patience,' I told him. 'You'll soon be ready to go'.

When Toby had been in his new home for about four days Wol abandoned his perch outside the French windows and installed himself on top of Toby's enclosure. How very touching, I thought – macho Wol going out of his way to bring comfort and companionship to this sad little waif. I should have known better; watching him strutting self-importantly across

171

the top of the enclosure, stopping from time to time to cat-call offensively to Toby, I realised that, far from bringing comfort, Wol's main aim was to goad Toby beyond endurance. 'Look at me,' he screeched gleefully, 'I'm free!' Toby eyed him dismally, his little monkey-face creased in an expression of profound melancholy, and chittered plaintively to himself.

Incensed, I hauled Wol off and took him back to his perch; ignoring his squawks of protestation I told him a few facts of Wol-life-as-it-was-going-to-be-in-the-not-too-distant-future. That his days as a house-owl, were numbered and that, as soon as I could bring myself to cut the umbilical cord, he was going to live outside and learn what owl-life was all about. His eyes widened in disbelief: What, sloppy old you throwing sweet, lovable old me out in the cold? That'll be the day! He had a point. I could see that I was going to have to do quite a bit of soul-searching and summon up reserves of steely resolve which I was pretty sure I didn't possess if I was ever to go through with my plans. But I was convinced that, in the long term, Wol would be happier living outside. Although he could never be released to live a truly natural life, he could have the next best thing – an outdoor enclosure that would give him closer contact with other wild creatures. But he would have to have a companion; he was much too sociable a creature to live outside on his own. There was no point in fostering an alliance with Toby as he would be going soon, leaving Wol bereft and alone. After examining my motives very, very carefully I decided that Wol's return to the semi-wild would have to wait until another permanently disabled owl came along. With that problem out of the way, at least for the time being, I concentrated on the immediate one – preparing Toby for his eventual release.

The first priority was to teach him to hunt for his own food, and this presented enormous difficulties. He was used to having his meals served up at regular intervals each day; he had absolutely no experience of catching live prey. If he was returned to the wild expecting a chunk of fur-trimmed beef or a defrosted chick to materialise under his nose twice a day he was in for a pretty lean time. On the other hand I knew there was no way I could bring myself to feed him live chicks or mice – it was one thing for him to hunt his own prey, but the idea of presenting him with live creatures to catch was too obscene even to think about. If Alf Turner, with his God-given gift for turning up at just the right moment, hadn't come to my aid I would probably still be racking my brain trying to find some means of resolving the situation that would be acceptable to all the parties concerned – the hunter, the hunted and the current food-provider.

'No problem,' said Alf when I told him my troubles. 'Go and get a piece of meat.' He tied the meat to the end of a length of string and instructed me to put it inside the enclosure. Holding the other end he stood a little distance away and drew the meat along the ground. Toby spotted it immediately; transfixed, he watched the somewhat erratic perambulations of the beef around the enclosure with saucer-wide eyes, head pivoting in an almost complete circle. Suddenly he swooped down and a grab for it, but it was gone. Alf, with incredible timing, had jerked it out of reach. I looked at Alf with bewilderment – why had he deprived Toby of his prey. 'Too easy' said Alf. 'He won't find mice and voles wandering around in circles under his nose in the wild. He's got to learn to outsmart them, to move faster than they do otherwise he'll never catch

anything.' He advised me to keep Toby on the hungry side and to feed him only moving prey.

Over the following weeks Toby and I practised every day and after a while I became almost as adept at manoeuvering the bait around the enclosure as he became at catching it. And then one day towards the end of summer I went into the enclosure and found him clutching the remains of a sparrow. My sadness at the untimely demise of the sparrow was somewhat tempered by joy at this evidence that Toby was capable of catching his own food. I decided that he was ready to go. Just before dusk I gave him what I tried not to think of as his Last Supper and opened the door of his enclosure. He showed absolutely no interest whatsoever. At half-hour intervals I went outside to see what, if anything, was happening, only to be confronted by a perplexed Toby, sitting on his barrel and wondering why he was suddenly the focus of all this noctural attention. But when I went out at dawn the next day his enclosure was empty – the bird had flown. I was delighted, truly I was. After all, that's what caring for sick creatures is all about – being able to return them to the wild. Why, then, did I have this niggling feeling of unease? At odd times during the day I found myself wondering where he was, how he was coping – was he hungry or cold, did he feel lonely and afraid out there in the harsh world on his own? This, of course, was what was troubling me – the uncertainty. If I could just know that he was all right I could finally cut the emotional cord.

Just before dark that night I went outside to bring Wol in. We were going through our usual nightly dialogue ('Time to come in, Wol.' 'No it's not.' 'It's almost dark.' 'Just another five minutes.' 'NOW!') when suddenly he gave an ear-splitting shriek and

started bouncing up and down on his perch. I followed his pop-eyed gaze and saw a Toby-shaped blob in the willow tree. With flapping wings the blob suddenly took off and swooped gracefully onto the top of the enclosure and I realised, to my joy, that it really was Toby. He fixed me with what I interpreted as an expectant eye then fluttered into the enclosure and took up his usual feeding position on top of the barrel. He had come home for supper. This was a real poser; if I fed him now he would take it for granted that he could always come back for a meal and would never learn to hunt for himself. On the other hand he was still new at the hunting game and might be having difficulty catching his own food. I decided to compromise; I gave him a little food to take the edge off his appetite but not enough to satisfy him completely. That way he would have both the incentive and the energy to hunt for prey. He gobbled down his meat, shot me a hopeful glance then, seeing that no more was forthcoming, flew out through the open door and soared across the paddock into the woods.

After that he came back every night and each time I reduced the amount of food until it was hardly worth his while coming back at all. But still he came, sometimes staying an hour or more, other times just circling overhead before taking off again. Wol looked forward to these visits enormously; every evening, just before dusk, he would scan the sky and the woods, all but twisting his little mophead off his non-existent neck. Suddenly he would start jumping up and down in a frenzy, chittering excitedly, and sure enough a moment later Toby would appear from nowhere. At first I though that Wol's behaviour was a reflection of his joy at seeing Toby again, and in a way it was. He was delighted to have someone to goad and insult and swear at, and Toby fitted the bill admirably. But I noticed that he no longer flaunted his 'freedom' in front of Toby; in contrast to his excitement at Toby's arrival, he watched his departure soberly and with a touch of wistfulness, and my heart ached for him. 'Never mind, little Wol,' I told him, 'sooner or later another disabled owl is going to turn up and you'll have a life-long companion.' He looked at me with wide-eyed astonishment. 'Another owl? Who needs another owl? I've got you. Where's my supper?'

ALL THE BEASTS OF THE FIELD
Sylvia Fenton

For thirty years, Sylvia Fenton nurtured a dream – a dream of leaving London, of buying a cottage in the country where she could indulge her passion for the countryside and provide a secure home for animals which needed help and protection.

It is a dream shared by thousands, but in her mid-forties Sylvia Fenton made it come true. At the end of a muddy, threequarter-mile cart track she found what she was looking for and, as if she had hung out a sign saying 'Vacancies for neglected animals', the beasts of the field began to arrive. Pooh the well-named ferret, escapologist donkeys, a hard-headed goat, Henrietta the unidentifiable fowl, a duck which fell in love with Sylvia Fenton's wellies and a lamb which insisted on sharing her bed: all were added to the existing household of five highly individual cats.

The animals are the real stars of the book, but Sylvia Fenton also writes of her discovery that country life is not all roses round the door – more like thistles round your ankles, nettles round your knees and mud up to your midriff. Fortunately she has the sense of the ridiculous which is essential for survival, and she writes with great humour of the trials, tribulations and catastrophes that can befall a transplanted townie.

Above all, the book is a sharing of the joy that Sylvia Fenton has found in the fulfilment of her dream and in caring for animals in need.

£7.95   162pp   925022 1